THIS PYRAMID

Building Relationships That Reflect the Light of His Spirit

LAURIE GANIERE

DEDICATION

To my love, my partner for life, next to Jesus, my best friend, Rick. I love you! Your patience with the process of this book has been never ending. Thank you for loving me unconditionally. You are an example of Jesus to me every day.

To the multitudes of you that have invested in this book through praying and fighting spiritual battles with me, I thank you. You're the best! I pray God's blessings on you!

LAURIE GANIERE

TABLE OF CONTENTS

LAURIE GANIERE

INTRODUCTION

"If you are filled with light, with no dark corners, then your whole life will be radiant, as though a floodlight were filling you with light." Luke 11:36 MSG

God calls us to relationships. Whether you are an introvert or extrovert, God calls us to relationships. He has put in the heart of every man, woman and child the need to be connected to Him and to others.

I believe there is a pyramid of relationships that God has ordained. When built correctly, we can celebrate the best in every relationship, and walk through the difficult times with trust that is built on the foundation of that pyramid.

It is my prayer that as you join me on this journey of looking at **THIS PYRAMID**, every relationship in your life will become richer. Whether married or single, CEO or just got a job at the bottom of the totem poll. Small business owner or stay at home parent. Church leader or just walked into the door of a church for the first time. Whether you are a Christian or not! Whether you come from a functional or dysfunctional family system. You will find a path to health in every relationship in your life, as long as **THIS PYRAMID** is built correctly.

That sounds like a tall order. We have probably all heard messages or read articles about pyramids and relationships. This one is different. I believe when we see the structure of **THIS PYRAMID**, and live it out the way God ordered, we will live well with every person in our life.

We will be better. Why? Because the light of His Spirit shines through us: *"If you are filled with light, with no dark corners, then your whole life will be radiant, as though a floodlight were filling you with light." Luke 11:36 MSG*

So, hang on. Here we go. God, marriage and family, church, friends, co-workers, neighbors and any I may have missed.

Laurie

PART ONE
The Foundation

LAURIE GANIERE

In the study of ancient pyramids, there are many theories on what pyramids were used for. But it is clear that the ancient Egyptians built pyramids to be tombs for the pharaohs and their queens. Inside the pyramids, along with their mummified remains, were their valuables as well. Often, those valuables were wrapped inside the mummified bodies. That sounds disgusting, but it's true.

So I would start out by saying that **THIS PYRAMID** also houses valuables, the valuables of the living, not the dead. There is no one dead in **THIS PYRAMID**, but very much alive. **THIS PYRAMID** is built with God as the foundation, and every other relationship is built upon Him. The Apostle Paul said in *1 Corinthians 3:16: "Don't you know that you yourselves are God's temple and that God's Spirit dwells in your midst?"* There is great value inside **THIS PYRAMID**. The incredible Holy Spirit of our very much alive God that lives inside of us! He changes every relationship that is built in **THIS PYRAMID**.

"If you are filled with light, with no dark corners, then your whole life will be radiant, as though a floodlight were filling you with light." Luke 11:36 MSG

The Shape

Wikipedia gives us a good picture of the shape of pyramids: "A **pyramid** (from Greek: πυραμίς pyramis)[1] [2] is a structure whose outer surfaces are triangular and converge to a single point at the top, making the shape roughly a pyramid in the geometric sense. The base of a pyramid can be trilateral, quadrilateral, or any polygon shape, meaning that a pyramid has at least three outer triangular surfaces (at least four faces including the base)."

For the sake of this book, **THIS PYRAMID** is trilateral. **THIS PYRAMID** has many layers, each one made of fine stone and mortar, to build a pyramid that will house His Spirit, shining out of every seam and stone and affecting every relationship and everyone in our sphere of influence.

So, let's begin with the foundational layer.

RELATIONSHIP WITH GOD

There is one relationship that is foundational in **THIS PYRAMID**. It is our relationship with God. If that relationship is not built correctly or missing completely, nothing else will be sustainable in **THIS PYRAMID**. Or if your God has a little "g", meaning He is not THE most important relationship in your life, that foundation will surely crumble in time, leaving every other relationship crashing around it, or struggling at best.

I have been in pastoral ministry for many years. I have consistently seen people struggle with marriages, families, friends, co-workers, bosses and church folk. Yes, church folk. Sometimes those are the worst. We will get to that later in the book.

At some point in my conversation with people, I often ask them to tell me about their relationship with God. Some are confounded that I would ask such a question when their marriage is in the ditch. They can't figure out why I would ask a question about God when it is their kids that are causing chaos all around. Some have gotten ticked at me when I suggest that their relationship with God just might be lacking, thus everything else is crashing around them. But it's true. Not always, I would never say always. But it bears the question. Is there something God is trying to tell us? Is He possibly trying to draw us closer to Him or get our attention about something? Again, that is not always the case, but many times, it is.

There are many dear friends who are walking in horrible trials in their lives and they are trusting God with every fiber of their being. They have learned to stay on the path of trusting the only One they can count on to use everything in their lives for good. Even when it all stinks and even when the trial is long and hard. Even when we love and serve God, life happens, and He uses all kinds of ways to speak life and hope into us. We'll talk more about that later as well.

There is one foundation, but trilateral, if you remember the shape. The first layer is represented by God the Father, God the Son, and God the Holy Spirit. The three corners of the triangular shape represent the triune God. One God, three in one, the Father, the Son, and the Holy Spirit.

If our relationship with God is secure, everything, every relationship built on top of it will be stronger. Even if relationships get messy, as we all know they do, the foundation is secure, and His Holy Spirit works to help us navigate those messy relationships in a way that God is glorified in and through it. You and I grow as we allow Him to shine in us first, through to those in the next layers of relationships.

This solid foundation is a relationship with God, through His Son, Jesus Christ. Here's the weird thing. We can't do anything to earn it. We can't do enough good stuff to make us good enough for Him to love us and welcome us into relationship with Him.

Ephesians 2:8-9 NIV "For it is by grace you have been saved, through faith _ and this is not from yourselves, it is the gift of God _ ⁹ not by works, so that no one can boast."

Grace means it's a free gift from God. A free gift that is available to all of us. You can never do enough good to make yourself good enough for God. Never!

The Bible says in **Romans 3:23 NIV**, *"all have sinned and fall short of the glory of God."* That means everyone. No one is exempt. Not you, not me, no one. We ALL have sin in our lives and without Him, there is a price to pay for our sin.

"For the wages of sin is death, but the gift of God is eternal life in Christ Jesus our Lord." Romans 6:23 NIV

It is not God's will for any of us to live outside His family. He wants a relationship with you and me so much that He did the unthinkable to make that possible. He sent His one and only Son to come down to this earth as a human being, 100% God yet 100% man, to pay the debt that you and I could never pay. Seriously, we have NO way of paying off this debt. He didn't owe a thing, yet He came to pay the debt that we owe.

One of the most familiar scriptures known to us is *John 3:16&17 NIV "For God so loved the world that he gave his one and only Son, that whoever believes in him shall not perish but have eternal life. For God did not send his Son into the world to condemn the world, but to save the world through him."*

Earlier on in that chapter, a man named Nicodemus came to Jesus late one night. He was tormented with one question. What must a man do to be saved? How do I come into a relationship with God? Jesus' response to Nicodemus was this: "you must be born again."

To say Nicodemus was freaked out is probably an understatement. I'm fairly sure it was a, "Wait! What?" kind of pause when Jesus said, "You must be born again." He asked Jesus how that was even possible. How can a man go back into his mother's womb and be born again? Jesus, the great teacher, went on to explain to Nicodemus that it is by grace (the free gift) through faith in Him. He told him that it was a spiritual birth, not another physical birth.

So the first question in looking at **THIS PYRAMID**, is this: have you been spiritually re-born? Have you accepted, by faith, Jesus Christ as your Lord and Savior? Have you ever asked Him to forgive you of your sin and help you live a life in His love, mercy and grace? Have you found new life in Jesus Christ?

My Story

I remember well when I first realized that I had a weight of sin. I had everything I needed in my life. I really didn't think I had any needs. My husband loved me, I had a beautiful baby daughter. My life was good, or so I thought. We had friends, we partied with our friends whenever we had the opportunity. Alcohol and drugs were no strangers to our home and lives.

Yet, at some point, I began to feel empty. Inside! Everything on the outside was good, but my insides were all messed up. I knew I needed something, but didn't know what. A cousin of mine began sharing some "religious" things with me. I always knew her to be a wonderful person. She was the "religious" one in the family. She loved us. I mean, really loved us. She never criticized our drinking and drugging. In fact, she used to stay with our daughter on an occasional night when we went out partying.

At the same time, *Jesus Christ Superstar* came out and caused quite a scene to many religious, and non-religious types. We were all in the "hippie" thing, so this musical was incredibly appealing to us. It raised questions in me that caused me to look seriously at who Jesus really was? Who was He? Is He really real and personal? Or is He just the guy we learned about in school?

See, as a child, I attended a Lutheran grade school and church. We were taught the Word of God. We memorized scripture, we memorized the deep theology in the old hymns. It was a wonderful education. Somewhere in it all though, I missed the relationship part of it. They did their job. It was I that missed it. I saw it as something we "do", rather than something we "become."

I remember at one point in my early 20's, I felt this huge, God sized hole in my heart. I was confused with all the *Jesus Christ Superstar* questions, and what I had been taught as a kid. The problem was I didn't KNOW Him. I knew who He was, but I just didn't KNOW Him. It was kinda like knowing the president. You know who he is, but you don't really KNOW him. That's the way it was with God. I didn't really KNOW Him.

So with my spiritual curiosity at an all time high, we began seeing things change in a BIG way in the lives of those around us. Things they used to do, they didn't do any more. They didn't criticize us for not doing them, but they didn't join us in our frivolous life any longer.

I remember one night, sitting at the kitchen table, playing with the Ouija Board. We were just having "fun." The Ouija Board is also known as the "spirit board or talking board." Participants place their fingers on the planchette, and it moves about to spell out answers to the questions you ask it. The problem is, it moves all by itself. Seriously – this is not for fun. It is a spiritually dangerous game. We were all feeling creeped out that this thing was actually working. Then right in the middle of the "game", my uncle came in. I learned earlier that he had accepted Christ and that his life was very different now. Well, I found out just how different it was. That planchette flew off the board and crashed into the cupboard. We never picked it up again. Scared the liver out of us all. As well it should have.

But as God is God, He connects the dots in everything in our lives. It was shortly after this, I was home with Rick and our daughter, and I was flipping through the TV channels and a Billy Graham Crusade came on. I started to change the channel, but something made me wait. As Rev. Graham was giving the altar call, and telling these people how much God loved them and accepted them right where they were, my heart fell into a puddle of despair. I couldn't understand why I felt this huge weight of sadness come over me. I started to cry. Immediately I got up and ran into the bathroom. Didn't want Rick to see me crying. I was pretty sure he would think I'd lost my mind.

Not long after that, my cousin invited us to a Sunday night service at Grace Assembly of God on 97th and Lisbon in Milwaukee. When we walked in, I'm sure we caused some kind of culture shock for this congregation. Our appearance was that of hippies, scruffy hair, Rick's flowing down his back, and mine doing the same. It was customary for me to wear a high waisted hippie dress and sandals. We felt we should mind our p's and q's, so we didn't drink or take any mind altering drugs before we went.

All that said, we walked in and these people loved on us. REALLY loved on us. They were kind. They were welcoming. I believe there's a big difference between being friendly and being welcoming. You can be friendly in saying hello to someone. But to be welcoming, requires much more. It requires engaging people in conversation and emotional connection. They spoke to us. Smiled, helped us find somewhere to sit. Showed us where the restrooms were. Took an interest in our baby. It felt odd. I wasn't used to that kind of treatment. I was fairly sure they would judge us and we just wouldn't fit in. I was flabbergasted that I was wrong.

The next Sunday, we went back. When we walked in the door, this dear little lady, who I soon learned was named Martha, gave me a warm smile, gave me a side hug, and said "I'm so glad you came again." I have to tell you I was shocked. I was overcome with emotion that someone truly cared about us. Her comment totally disarmed me, and my attitude about not fitting in. Little Martha disarmed me. Jesus disarmed me through this little lady.

That night, when the pastor gave the altar call, I got up from my seat and made my way down to the altar. I had no idea what I was doing. I just knew what I felt was so deep in my soul, that I just needed to do what he said.

I knew Jesus was calling me, Laurie Ganiere, to come to Him.

That night began a journey, a journey of following Jesus. Today, it's been well over forty years since that journey began. I learned that I was now HIS child. I was washed clean of the sin that separated me from Him. I became a member of His family. I learned that I didn't have to hide from Him. I learned that His love was so deep for me that He accepted me just as I am. I learned that my shame and guilt were gone, never to hold me back from Him again. He paid a price for me that He didn't owe, for the debt that I had no way to pay. I am forgiven and free. I learned early on that Jesus had a plan for me.

His promises are amazing to everyone that is part of this great family. One great promise is found in *Jeremiah 29:11-13 NIV "For I know the plans I have for you," declares the Lord, "plans to prosper you and not to harm you, plans to give you hope and a future. Then you will call on me and come and pray to me, and I will listen to you. You will seek me and find me when you seek me with all your heart."*

Your Story

If you haven't ever received His free gift of salvation, don't wait. He is calling you too. The foundation of your life will be strong and able to endure anything life has for you if you walk this journey with Him. He loves you. He really loves you.

All you have to do is talk to Him. Tell Him that you open the door of your heart and invite Him in. There's this picture that I've seen in a lot of places - churches, peoples homes, Christian stores - it's a picture of Jesus standing at a door and knocking. It's based on the Scripture in Revelation where Jesus said He's standing at the door and knocking. If you open the door, He will come in and have relationship with you.

That door is your heart. If you look at that picture, there's no doorknob on that door. Jesus is standing outside, simply knocking. He can't open it Himself. He gave you a free will to open that door. When you open it and invite Him in, He will come in and forgive you of everything and anything you've ever done, said or thought. He just wants a relationship with you. HE LOVES YOU. HE REALLY LOVES YOU.

All you have to do is say a prayer something like this: *God, I want to know You. I believe in You. I want to have a relationship with You. I'm lost without You. I ask You to forgive my sin. Come in to my heart and life and be my Savior, and my Friend. Help me to live for You the rest of the days of my life. Thank you Jesus that You gave Your life for me, that I could be free. In Jesus Name, Amen!*

This is the beginning of your spiritual birth. God loves you and has a plan for your life that is far beyond what you could ever think or imagine. You are a part of the family of God. If you don't have a church, look for one that preaches a message like this one. I am part of the Assemblies of God, but there are so many good churches out there. Find a good church that preaches the Gospel. Begin to grow in Him. Serve Him. Get yourself a Bible and begin reading in the New Testament. Read a chapter every day. Ask God to begin revealing Himself to you every day.

This is the first layer, the foundation of **THIS PYRAMID**.

Open Your Eyes

So, in talking about being "born again", I want to share with you a deep truth, that is foundational to **THIS PYRAMID**, about the great love of God. After our seventh granddaughter Carina was born, the hospital staff put her tiny little body on the warming cart. She was crying ever so hard. Her daddy, our son Christopher, walked over to her and said, "I'm here baby. I'm right here. Daddy's here." That tiny shivering little one stopped crying when she heard the voice of her daddy. She recognized his voice because he used to talk to her a lot when she was in the womb. She recognized his voice.

A short time after she was consoled, he walked back over to his wife, as they were tending to her following birth. Little Carina once again started crying, so very hard, shaking and crying. Christopher once again walked over to the cart with his precious daughter on it and began talking to her again. Once again, she quieted when she heard his voice.

Then he said the most amazing thing happened. She was quieted, and he continued talking to her and said these words: "I love you baby. I love you. Mama and I love you." As soon as she heard her daddy say, "I love you," she opened her little baby eyes and looked at him for the first time. She looked squarely at him with a gaze that will last for eternity.

A short time after arriving home from the hospital, they were looking at some things online relative to birth. They found a Michael Jr. video, a Father's Day video, that he told the exact same story about him and his daughter. Watch it on YouTube. I promise you, it will blow you away. Same experience.

So, what's the point? Please know friends that your Father loves you. When you get that deep into your soul, it changes you forever. Because of the depth of His love, unconditional love, shame disappears and we have the ability to open our eyes, and see Him. You are accepted by Him! You are secure in Him. You have purpose and identity in Him. Open your eyes! Like our little baby granddaughter did, open your eyes. He is telling you today that He loves you. He wants you to know that clearly, so that you will have the ability to walk in faith, knowing He is all you need. Your foundation in **THIS PYRAMID** is built on that.

You are His child – a son or daughter of the King of Kings. The God that loved you THAT much has promises for you that are great – they start today and never end, on through eternity. It is on that love, that EVERYTHING in our life is built, on that foundation, Christ in you. He's all you need.

Foundation in Everyday Life

Jesus had much to say about foundation:

"I will show you what it's like when someone comes to me, listens to my teaching, and then follows it. ⁴⁸It is like a person building a house who digs deep and lays the foundation on solid rock. When the floodwaters rise and break against that house, it stands firm because it is well built. ⁴⁹But anyone who hears and doesn't obey is like a person who builds a house right on the ground,

without a foundation. When the floods sweep down against that house, it will collapse into a heap of ruins." Luke 6:47-49 NLT

The very foundation of our lives must be built on Him if we intend to be strong. The foundation in **THIS PYRAMID** must be built on Him or every other relationship in our life will collapse in time. Everything we need is found in Him and everything in our life will be in order if it's built on Him.

That puzzles a great number of people. Some people have foolishly said "I don't need to work a job if God is gonna supply everything I need." One thing you need to know right from jump is this: God will never contradict His Word. His Bible is His Word. Yes it does say that He will supply all of our needs – according to HIS riches in glory. It also says that we must work if we want to eat. So if you think you can be a sluggard and do nothing, think again. God calls us to partner with Him in everything. And that includes work.

God supplies through a variety of means: some of which are supernatural, and others are seemingly natural. Some of those come through others, and some come supernaturally through Him. No matter the path of provision, ultimately they are from Him.

GOD GIVEN NEEDS

There are needs that we all have as human beings, and typically, we look to other people and things to fill those needs. God is the one who wants to meet every need in our life, but most of us have a hard time figuring out how He does that. We have a hard time wrapping our heads around what it really means. Consequently, we look to other people and things to meet them.

Let me emphasize that God has given us these needs. He created us to have them. Any time we look to other people or other things to fill those needs, we have very short-term success, and will once again be empty and dry. The reason? Because people and things are not meant to, nor are they capable of meeting those needs.

When we look to other people or things to meet those needs that are not theirs to fill, this is known as the **The Principal of Transference.** They will die trying to meet our needs, and we will continue to be dry and thirsty.

If it's stuff, substances, or things, again, we will have short term relief, and always come back around to needing more and more of stuff, substances or things. Because our STUFF isn't meant to fill us! Only God can. Does this sound repetitive? It is – because it's a BIG DEAL that so many people struggle with.

If you can GET this, you will see why it is so critical that your relationship with God is built right and is solid.

God created every human being with four basic needs:

ACCEPTANCE - God loves you and accepts you. As we spoke about before, He loved you enough that He sent His Son to die for you so that you could then have a relationship with Him. He loves you and accepts you right where you are. Stop looking to others to find acceptance. When you find it in Him, you will see how quickly you can relax, and not try to extract it from other people or things. Do you see why this is the foundation in **THIS PYRAMID**?

PURPOSE - God has a purpose for you. *Jeremiah 29:11-13 NIV "For I know the plans I have for you," declares the Lord, "plans to prosper you and not to harm you, plans to give you hope and a future. [12]Then you will call on me and come and pray to me, and I will listen to you. [13]You will seek me and find me when you seek me with all your heart."*
When you look to Him, He will make His path clear and you won't continually live in wonder of what your purpose is. You will simply do the next thing, and walk out day to day on the path that He lays out for you. He will walk with you in discovering His purpose in your life. If you

continually look to others to make it clear, your foundation will soon begin wobbling. Your foundation will crumble if it is others you look to for purpose.

SECURITY – you are secure in Him. *Romans 8:38 NLT "And I am convinced that nothing can ever separate us from God's love. Neither death nor life, neither angels nor demons, neither our fears for today nor our worries about tomorrow _ not even the powers of hell can separate us from God's love."*

Married couples, you will see in the next section that you can't continually look to your spouse for your security. You will become needy to them and ultimately begin to be unattractive to them, as you suck the life out of them. Your security is found in God and in Him alone. If you are a woman, your security cannot be fully found in your husband. No matter how many doors he opens for you, or how safe he makes you feel during crisis or storms. Your security must be found in the King of Kings and the Lord of Lords. The one that holds this universe in His hands has you tenderly, yet securely in His palm.

IDENTITY - *Jeremiah 1:5 NLT "I knew you before I formed you in your mother's womb. Before you were born I set you apart and appointed you…"* **Your identity is as a child of God. And there's a whole Bible that gives you the details of what that all means.**

31

When I think of identity, and feeling secure in "whose" you are, I often think of the children whose parents are in the White House. There are many pictures of former US Presidents with their children in the Oval Office with them. Because of WHOSE they are, they have access to their dad unlike anyone else.

I remember when I was a youngster, former President John F. Kennedy had two children, John and Caroline, who were shown sitting under their dad's desk and standing around during important meetings. Because of "whose" they are, they were allowed the privilege of being in the Oval Office. At the end of the day, John Kennedy was "dad" before he was President of the United States of America.

Because your identity is in God Almighty, you can relax and enjoy Him and the life you have in Him. He knew you before you were born. You are His child. You can never be a pain to Him by bursting into an important meeting. There will never be a time when He will brush you away. Your identity is in a God that loves you. His love for you transcends any other love that anyone or anything on this earth could ever hold for you. Stop looking for love and identity in people or things. Your identity is found in Him.

So, relax, bask in His love. You're a child of the King!

Walking in Faith for a Secure Foundation

Faith — a word that gets bantered around quite a bit. What is faith? *"Faith shows the reality of what we hope for; it is the evidence of things we cannot see. Through their faith, the people in days of old earned a good reputation." Hebrews 11:1-2 NLT*

We say we walk by faith. We sing about being people of great faith because He is faithful. Real faith is believing even though we cannot see. Based on the foundation of who HE is, not on who WE are. That's why **THIS PYRAMID** is different than the others of ancient days.

They used to build pyramids in such a way that the heaviest materials were used on the bottom, to sustain the weight of the remainder of the structure. The same is true of **THIS PYRAMID**. The strength of this structure is in the foundation.

The higher they went in building that structure, the finer, more beautiful materials were used for all to see. **THIS PYRAMID**, however, along with the strength of the foundation, also has the most valuable and finest at the bottom. His precious Holy Spirit, shines through every layer and relationship in our lives. Because of who HE is, we can have confidence and faith, that what He says will be. We have faith in His ability that no matter what is coming our way, in every relationship, we will view everything and everyone through the lens of faith in Him.

Hebrews 11 goes on to talk about great people of faith: Abel, Enoch, Noah, Abraham, Sarah, Isaac, Jacob, Joseph, Moses, Rahab and so many more. Because they believed God as their firm foundation, they faced every obstacle as an opportunity for God to move mountains on their behalf.

> *Hebrews 11:1 NLT*
> *"Faith is the confidence that what we hope for will actually happen; it gives us assurance about things we cannot see."*

We too can be people of such great faith. Do I see obstacles to stop me, or do I see opportunities for God to show up and do amazing things? Even when we struggle we must remind ourselves that this is one more opportunity for God to be God.

As Christians, no matter where we look, there is a lot said about faith. In our everyday life, we walk in faith all the time. We put faith in our cars, clothes, people, jobs and so much more. We have faith that when we get in our car it's going to start. I even put a certain amount of faith in my jeans when I put them on. That they are made well and will hold this chubby body and not split the seams. We have faith that people will do what they should – or... not so much.

Real faith, however, is based on things we can't see. Not calculated risk.

If I put the money in the bank, I trust it will be there when I go to get it. That's trust. I had to put the money in there, and trust that the bank will keep it for me til I need it. It's an investment.

Trust and faith are related, but not the same. Faith is very different. Faith is having confidence based on what we CANNOT see. From God's Word, faith is not based on proof, but rather a reliance on who HE is and what HE promises.

Hebrews 11:1 NLT "Faith is the confidence that what we hope for will actually happen; it gives us assurance about things we cannot see."

I don't have any proof — yet I believe that something is going to happen, or that something is true. That's faith. It's not blind faith, it's based on His Word.

I believe that in **THIS PYRAMID**, our faith is crucial to maintain a healthy balance in day to day life. I lean on His Word and when I take my eyes off Him and His Word, my faith wavers, and even crashes. What causes me to waiver? What causes me to take my eyes off of Him? Why do I take my eyes off of Him? Maybe, just maybe, it is what I call "faithsquashers." There are four things that will keep us from walking in faith and take our eyes off of Jesus, the Author and Finisher of our faith, and place them squarely on ourselves. Sadly, we don't often see them, until they truly have squashed our faith.

There are four "faithsquashers" that I have identified. As you read them, you may find one or more of them that have hindered your faith.

FAITHSQUASHER NO. 1 – FEAR

Fear keeps us from having confidence of what we hope for. Fear is believing a distorted view of God, circumstances and the promises in God's Word.

Faith is believing in what we cannot see. Fear squashes faith. It distorts reality according to the Word of God.

Fear doesn't come from God. Power, love and a sound mind come from God, but certainly not fear. *"For God has not given us a spirit of fear, but of power and of love and of a sound mind." 2 Timothy 1:7 NKJV*

If you are struggling with faith, check your fear-factor. If you feel fear, that's not power. If you struggle with fear, that's not love. Fear will leave you feeling like you don't have a sound mind. It throws off your ability to hear from God and walk in the power and authority He has for you.

Fear keeps us focused on ourselves or on obstacles. When I am focused on myself or others I cannot see God clearly.

I heard of a well-known evangelist who struggled all night in prayer. He was in a hotel room, and awoke to see a shadow flying around the room. He immediately got up, and began to pray fervently, battling some distorted figure that he assumed was the devil there to destroy him. He literally stormed the gates of heaven most of the night. As the sun began to rise, he saw that his coat was hanging on a coat rack, and was blowing in the wind. It was the shadow of the wind that he thought was the enemy there to destroy him. He had a distorted view of reality. He was brave enough to tell the story, an incredible example of fear taking over our life.

Through his story, we can see that sometimes we see distortions that cause fear to rise up. I heard a great acronym for fear: F-false, E-evidence, A-appearing, R-real.

> **F - False**
> **E - Evidence**
> **A - Appearing**
> **R - Real**

Fear doesn't come from God. Power, love and sound mind are what is produced when we walk in faith and trust that God is who He says He is and will do what He says He will do.

So in choosing to squash fear today, you must make a decision to believe truth. Faith is a choice to believe the truth. It is not a feeling, it's a choice. What will you choose - faith or fear? Faith is life giving. Fear is life destroying, or diverting our attention away from the life giver.

FAITHSQUASHER NO. 2 - COMPARISON

Comparison is something we all do. If you think you don't — think again. To some degree, we all do.

I remember one morning sitting at my piano. Seriously, I don't play well. I played accordion as a kid (don't you tell a soul I said that), and I often joke that I know just enough about the piano to be dangerous.

Truthfully, I only play for Jesus and me. Sometimes my husband hears me, but that's it. It's just me and Jesus time. I have a wonderful friend, David Kaap, who is one of the most skilled, anointed pianist and worship leaders that I know. To say I admire him is an understatement. Well, one day I was lamenting — "Help me God - I just wish I could play like David. If I could only worship you like that God." What God said to me next, brought me to my knees with tears flowing. He said: "Laurie — when you play for Me, I hear a symphony."

Those words from my Father were like a fresh drink of water to my soul. To hear Him say "when you do this for Me, I hear a symphony." I realized that comparison really kept my eyes focused on my inadequacies and not on my ability to use what I had to worship Him. Every fiber of our being as believers is to live a life of worship using everything and anything He gives us. When I use it for Him, He hears a symphony.

We compare everything in our lives. We compare our families, our spouses, our cars, our houses, our clothes, whatever. If only I could be like that, then my life would be so much better. Sadly not only does it squash your faith, but it keeps your eyes on you and what you don't have.

If you continually see the success of others as a threat to you, it will continually be a noose around your neck and you will have constant feelings of failure. Who can live like that for long. And you certainly can't walk in faith to be all He has created you to be cuz your vision is so clouded.

We just talked about fear. While fear keeps us focused on a distorted reality, comparison keeps us focused on what we don't have. We become selfish, envious, and never realize our full potential in Christ, all because we don't see ourselves as good enough.

You will never walk in faith if you live a life of comparison. **Comparison is a cancer to contentment.**

Like cancer eats away at our body, comparison eats away at our contentment and destroys our faith.

Robert Madu says: "Comparison will consistently cloud the clarity of God's call on your life."

You can't see God and His call when you consistently compare yourself, your family, your ministry or anything else.

"We do not dare to classify or compare ourselves with some who commend themselves. When they measure themselves by themselves and compare themselves with themselves, they are not wise."
2 Corinthians 10:12 NIV

We need to kill our comparisons – or our comparisons will kill our faith walk. Why? Because comparison is a three-headed monster: it leads to jealousy, selfishness and feelings that we will never quite measure up. It's more serious than we've ever realized.

"Jealousy is truly resenting God's goodness in other people's lives and ignoring God's goodness in our own life." - Craig Groeschel from his book #*struggles*.

Listen to this: *"But if you are bitterly jealous and there is selfish ambition in your heart, don't cover up the truth with boasting and lying. For jealousy and selfishness are not God's kind of wisdom. Such things are earthly, unspiritual, and demonic. For wherever there is jealousy and selfish ambition, there you will find disorder and evil of every kind." James 3:14-16 NLT*

Comparison has its roots in jealousy and selfishness. We must cut it off! You can never win comparing yourself to someone else.

Craig Groeschel *#struggles*: "Identify bad influences and celebrate others successes. Suffocate the flames of envy with a blanket of gratitude. Cultivate gratitude!"

The only way to squash comparison is to begin to cultivate an attitude of gratitude. God has created you to be YOU. In you are all the gifts and abilities He designed you to have. Celebrate the gifts He's given others and celebrate the gifts He's given you.

To walk in power and faith – celebrate God's goodness in others, and rejoice in all He has made you to be. If you haven't discovered your own gifts yet, talk to your Pastor or Ministry Leader. I'm guessing they can set you on a path to discover them.

Rejoice! Celebrate! Squash any hint of comparison in your life.

FAITHSQUASHER NO. 3 – UNFORGIVENESS

This is a tough topic. I understand. Please don't check out. Please don't close the book or flip to the next chapter. This is a tough subject. Even my computer doesn't like it. Every time I type unforgiveness, it underlines it in red telling me there's something wrong with the word. Think not? Try it.

Even online dictionaries don't have a definition for unforgiveness. It says "do you mean 'forgive'?" You can find "unforgivingness", but not "unforgiveness." There are times in our lives that we act like there isn't even a word like that – or like it's a "bad word" that doesn't show up in the dictionary. Like some of those words you learned in the back alley as a kid, and you were later taught were wrong by someone in authority, or one of your parents.

Even though the word unforgiveness doesn't show up in the dictionary, you can find countless authors that have written wonderful works on the subject. Some on how toxic it is, some giving you steps to overcoming, and still others to help you see what forgiveness IS and what it is NOT.

In our heart of hearts, we know unforgiveness has grave consequences, but we continue to nurse our wounds, find ways to justify not forgiving someone for the wrong that was done to us. Truth be known, it will squash your faith, and the consequences to you are severe.

Matthew 6:14-15 NLT "If you forgive those who sin against you, your heavenly Father will forgive you. But if you refuse to forgive others, your Father will not forgive your sins."

In **Matthew 18**, Jesus talks about the man that was forgiven much yet refused to forgive the debt that another man owed him. Jesus showed clearly the consequence of such actions. When we refuse to forgive someone, the consequences fall on us.

Jeanne Mayo is an internationally known Youth Leader. She is forever young, and has been successfully raising up youth leaders for many years. I once heard Jeanne say **"unforgiveness is allowing a person to live in your head rent-free."** It costs you everything, utilities, wear and tear on the property, noise, dollars to pay your mortgage, but costs them nothing.

A Laurie Ganiere-ism:
"Unforgiveness corrodes the container that carries it."

The cost of unforgiveness is too great. It's a choice. It's not saying what they did was OK or right. It's choosing to not hold their sin against them any longer. It's a decision to release them from the debt they owe us for the wrong.

Jesus never says sin is ok and doesn't ask us to either. But when we come to Him, He forgives us and His Word tells us He throws it as far as the east is from the west –

and He remembers it no more. I believe He says that He throws it as far as the east is from the west because you can't measure that. You can measure north and south. If you are going north, you can only do that so long, and eventually you are going south. If you are going south, there will come a point that you will now be going north. But that will never happen if you are going east. There will never be a time that you are then going west. Impossible.

God never holds our sin against us, and will never bring it up again. He throws it as far as the east is from the west – and He remembers it no more. It does not mean He has a bad memory, rather it means He chooses to never bring it up again. The debt has been paid, stamped on the invoice "paid in full." It's over.

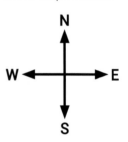

Choosing to forgive someone is between you and God. Rarely is it necessary to tell someone you forgive them. When we choose to tell them, unsolicited, what we're really doing is trying to extract some acknowledgment that what they did was wrong. Trying to get some "payment," if you will, from them for what they did to you. That's not forgiveness, that's vindication. That's not throwing it as far as east is from the west...and remembering it no more.

People have asked me throughout the years, "How do you do that? How do you walk that out?" I made it my motto years ago that "I will never give them an opportunity to say I dumped on them." I will always respond with respect, grace and forgiveness. I will leave the rest with God. Is it hard? Sometimes, yes. But it's a choice we make, every time it comes around again. Forgiving someone is rarely a one-time decision. Depending on the depth of the hurt or injury, we may have to make that choice every day. Choose to forgive. The further we get from the hurt, after healing starts to occur, it becomes less and less that we are faced with that hurt.

Now, please know that forgiveness and boundaries are two separate issues. I can forgive completely and still have a boundary in my life that I will not allow bad behavior to be given to me. Example of someone who has lived with abuse: you can forgive the abuser, but your boundaries dictate that you will not allow that person to abuse you again. If you have a problem with any kind of boundary issues, I strongly encourage you to pick up a great book by Drs. Henry Cloud and John Townsend called *Boundaries*.

Forgiveness is a choice – so is walking in faith. But if you refuse to forgive, you will also not be forgiven. A cost to your soul, not theirs.

Also, your unforgiveness will indeed squash your faith. The two can't co-exist. Make that decision today. Move on in faith. Ask God to help you walk in forgiveness. He understands. He forgave you.

The light of the precious Holy Spirit will continue to shine through you as you walk in forgiveness.

If you continue to struggle with forgiveness, I strongly encourage you to pick up the book by RT Kendall called *Total Forgiveness*. It is one of the greatest resources I've ever seen to help people understand what forgiveness is, what it is not, and how to walk in it as a believer. RT Kendall has also written another book called *How to Totally Forgive Yourself*. If you or someone you love is struggling with unforgiveness, take advantage of these two wonderful resources.

FAITHSQUASHER NO. 4 – "LOOKING FOR LOVE IN ALL THE WRONG PLACES"

In the last three sections, we have looked at three things that keep us from walking in faith. We long to be called people of faith, but we struggle with fear, comparison and unforgiveness. It is my prayer that the last three have helped you at some level to conquer those things that have bound you or those you love.

The fourth and final one we will talk about is **insecurities, or looking for love in all the wrong places.** Even seemingly strong and secure men and women have dealt with this at some level, at some time in their lives.

God has created each one of us with needs. As I said earlier, the REAL reasons God gave us those needs is that He is the only one that can fill them. He desires to have an intimate relationship with each of us, thus He gave us each needs that only He can meet.

The problem is, you and I occasionally try to get these needs met by someone or something other than God.

If we're married, we think our spouse is to meet all our needs. If we're not married, we think other people or other things will meet them.

Sadly, many deny they have these needs, yet they continue down a path that leads them to emptiness at the end. They run hard and fast, and still end up empty. Trying to get a drink of water, but the well is dry.

The enemy tricks us by taking things we enjoy or things we like and causes us to look there for satisfaction. In the end, they wind up sucking the life from us. And we continue to feel a loss and emptiness and don't know why.

One of the things about insecurity that we have to know is this: God loves you. He loves you and wants you to be secure in that. His well is full of refreshing water, and is life-giving, unlike anything else we could ever look to.

Part of the problem is that we don't really believe that He loves us. As women, it can be an easier leap, because we are usually more emotionally sensitive than guys. However, because of that, she can also try to find someone to meet those needs in other relationships and end up empty and emotionally drained and dry.

Guys, you have to know how much God loves you. He has hard wired you as a man, to understand His love, maybe a little different than a woman. But you too, may seek to get that need filled with other relationships, be it people or things. You too will remain dry and continually thirsty for that which only God can give.

The Foundation – *THIS PYRAMID*

Every other relationship in your life is impacted by your foundation. If it is solidly on Christ, other relationships, be it spouse, family, friends, church family, neighbor or co-workers, have a greater chance of success.

If our foundation is not solid in Him, we struggle, we fight, we can't find peace, we place trust in others and are continually disappointed. We foster pride, keeping us from any healthy relationships, and place the blame on everyone around us.

We face this cycle of madness over and over. Alone, insecure, with lack of purpose, not knowing "whose" we are. Yet we are tricked in to thinking we have it all.

But in Him, we can do all things, we can foster healthy relationships, and we know without a doubt, there is nothing that can separate us from Him.

Yes, the success or failure of every relationship in your life will rest on what you chose to do with Jesus. Is He your Lord and Savior? Or is He simply someone you know about, but you don't really know Him. He wants you to know Him. He wants to walk with you every day.

If you look at the history of pyramids, the finest of materials was put at the top, where they could shine and be on display for people to see for miles. In **THIS PYRAMID**, the finest materials are in the foundation. The materials used, will radiate through every other relationship in our lives. His Holy Spirit, coming through every relationship built on top. With the rich Holy Spirit flowing in, through and out of every level of **THIS PYRAMID**. So, what have YOU done with Jesus? Is HE your rock, your foundation? If there is anything standing between you and Him, settle it today.

Maybe you've looked to others to meet needs only He can meet. Maybe you've allowed some faithsquashers to get in the way of that relationship.

Whatever it is, I promise you this. He would say to you — *"Open your eyes. I love you. Let Me be the firm foundation in your life. I promise you — You and I will walk this road together. You will shine brightly with My strength, wisdom and power. You will affect everyone and everything in your sphere of influence. Why? Because your life will reflect Me. I love you. Open your eyes."*

PART TWO
Marriage and Family

LAURIE GANIERE

Whether you are married or not, this section is critical. It is layer number two, Marriage and Family. Even if you're not married, you have a family. You may not like them much, but you still have a family. Or, you may have a wonderful relationship with your family.

For the record, I believe that every family has a certain level of dysfunction. It's just a matter of how much. Part of the problem with dysfunction is that many of us live in it so long that we don't even realize how funky it really is. But for someone to look from the outside, they can see the funky mess we call family. Even so, you're still family, right?

As a Christian, we have the responsibility to our spouse and family to be the hands, feet, and voice of the God that loves them and died for them just as He did for you. Your first responsibility is to your family. And they are also the hardest to love at times. And for the light of the Holy Spirit to shine up through you into this next layer can prove to be the biggest challenge.

Even if things are well with your marriage and or family, there are things you can learn about how to be the extension of Christ to them in a way that makes a difference. If you think it's all good and there is nothing for you to learn, think again. There is always something for us to learn, especially ways for us to be a better representation of Christ, the light that shines up from your foundation. Remember, the foundation will be strong if God is the foundation of your pyramid. His Holy Spirit shines through the believer to EVERY person in your family. Again, I know, it's HARD.

Even if you're adopted, you may not know your biological family, but those that chose you to be a part of their forever family are yours to call your own.

There may be some of you that have suffered abuse in your family. Maybe you had family that was supposed to protect you from an abuser and did not. Consequently, you have a warped perception of what a Godly, loving family could be, and can't even imagine what that might look like, much less feel like. Later on in this section, I address abuse in a much deeper way. But you must know that God loves you.

THIS PYRAMID, Layer Two

As we talked earlier, **THIS PYRAMID** is built on that firm foundation of the Father, Son and Holy Spirit shining into every relationship in our lives, up through every layer after it. The first place it is seen is in marriage and family, the people that are closest to us.

If the foundation is **not** strong, your marriage and family stand a good chance of crumbling at some point in time. I wish I could tell you that if both husband and wife are Christians then there will be no issues in your marriage. That the love of Christ will shine through you both and it will all be as God planned. That is what is SUPPOSED to happen. Truth be known, you and I are imperfect human beings, sinful people, and make some pretty crumby choices that affect everyone in our lives, and our spouse or family members are the first to see that truth lived out.

MARRIAGE MATTERS

Rick and I teach Marriage Matters Seminars. We tell couples that there are common lies the enemy tells married people. Some of them include:

- **"Nobody has the kind of problems we have."**
  Lie #1. This lie will keep you isolated from the help you really need. Anything that lives in isolation will eventually die. Or, another way to look at it is this: if you cover up an infection without treatment, it multiplies, and the spread of disease goes rampant. Eventually, death will occur.
  People DO have the problems you have.
  Ecclesiastics 1:9 NIV tells us that *"there is nothing new under the sun."* What you are experiencing in your marriage, many others have already experienced, or surely will. If you will recognize that, there is help for you. If, however, you isolate, you

give room for the devil to inflict more infection into your already troubled relationship.

- Another lie is **"I made a mistake, we're just not meant to be together."** The next float in that parade is, "because I made a mistake that gives me license to get a divorce. It was just a mistake, right?" People make mistakes all the time. So, divorce is the next step. Never mind that you took a vow. Never mind that you said "til death do us part." *Ecclesiastes 5:5 NIV* says *"It is better not to make a vow than to make one and not fulfill it."* All you're really saying is, "I don't want to do the work it will take to make this right and God honoring." It's just easier to agree with the lie that I, or we, made a mistake.

- Or **"I didn't listen to God. This wasn't His will."** My sassy response would be something like this: "Seriously, you're gonna put this on God? You took a vow." So if you blame God, it relieves you of responsibility to do anything? See bullet point above. You've just made up your mind that you're not going to do what it takes. Never mind that you took a VOW before the **same** God that you are **now** **blaming**.

- **"Counseling won't help. I'm not gonna see a shrink or a Pastor."** What you're really saying is that you don't want to run the risk of anyone telling you that you might be wrong. Mostly because then you will have to take responsibility. Your pride will continue to tell you that YOU know what's best for you, and it's not this marriage.

Remember your foundation: the Spirit of God IN you. His Holy Spirit shines into every relationship in your life. Or it should be. When you make up your mind that you are not getting Godly help, you are putting a cover over the Holy Spirit, and truly saying "can't shine through me today, sorry."

Do you believe the Word of God? Do you believe that in it is truth? If you do, you must know that God's Word promises you so much help. Think about the following scriptures a minute:

- *Romans 8:28 NIV "And we know that in all things God works for the good of those who love him, who have been called according to his purpose."* You are called according to His purpose. Will you allow His purpose to be worked in your heart? In your marriage? In your family?
- *Proverbs 15:22 NIV "Plans fail for lack of counsel."*

- *Proverbs 11:14 NIV "For lack of guidance a nation falls, but victory is won through many advisors."*

God promises that there is help. Seek the help. The longer that we isolate, our thinking becomes upside down, or at the very least lop sided. Our spiritual equilibrium gets thrown off when we want our own way and refuse help. What seems right is really wrong, and what seems wrong is really right. Your spiritual equilibrium is upside down and you can't trust your own heart or thinking. That is precisely what happens when you isolate yourself.

To get it right side up, seek God and those that He has placed in your life to help you. It's never too late. Only seek out those that are FOR marriage. Don't believe the lie that divorce is your only solution.

The Beginning

One of the first things we have to deal with in our seminars is to win over the one that doesn't want to be there. That might be true of the one reading this book as well. So indulge me for a minute. There is a percentage of people that come for one of the following reasons:

- Their spouse strong-armed or threatened them.
- Their spouse was holding something over their head to get them there, YOU OWE ME.

- OR their spouse promised them something if they would just go to this seminar, so they come with the proverbial chip on their shoulder.

Our first job is to be real and vulnerable to the couples that come. We help them to laugh, we show them our own stupidity and the crazy lives that most married people have. We have learned over the years to laugh at ourselves. We've taught our kids to laugh at themselves so it doesn't hurt so much when others laugh AT you. Please know this - it wasn't easy to laugh at ourselves in the early days of marriage. When you'd rather high five someone in the forehead because you're ticked isn't when you want to laugh with each other. I'm talking figuratively friends. We get so mad that finding something to laugh at is so far out of the realm of possibility. It takes an immense amount of social intelligence to know when you've reached that point where it's ok.

We've learned that words matter. We've learned that eye rolls matter. We've learned that "dragon breath" matters (you know the deep breath followed by a long drawn out breath of disgust). Things that we do and say to each other can cause an immense amount of damage that can remain hidden for some time.

We, however, can be so selfish, wanting our own way, that we just allow words to come out that hurt. There are times that we say hurtful things and then after the fact, say something like: "I don't know where that came from. I didn't really mean that." Truth be known, if we have an inkling of what the Word of God says, we DO know where it comes from. *Matthew 15:18 NIV "But the things that come out of a person's mouth come from the heart, and these defile them."* Before they come out of our mouths, they are first in our hearts.

What comes out of our mouths, and out in our actions, starts in our heart. The scripture also says that it is our responsibility to guard our hearts. Our hearts, without a relationship with God, are so much darker than we think. Even with a relationship with God, we must continue to go back to Him and ask Him to do a heart check. We must ask Him to cleanse us that we would be a clear reflection of Him in every relationship.

People work so hard to change their behaviors. **They think that if they can only control that stupid behavior, that their heart would be better and their relationship with God would be good. _That's backwards._** Everything starts with 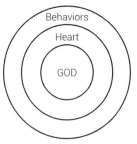 our relationship with God. He changes our hearts, gives us the charge to GUARD our hearts, because it is from there that our behaviors flow. So our responsibility, whether it is in marriage, or family, or most any relationship, is to make sure that we guard our heart.

Proverbs 17:27 NIV "The one who has knowledge uses words with restraint, and whoever has understanding is even-tempered."

Proverbs 16:24 NIV "Gracious words are a honeycomb, sweet to the soul and healing to the bones."

Ephesians 4:29 NIV "Do not let any unwholesome talk come out of your mouths, but only what is helpful for building others up according to their needs, that it may benefit those who listen."

Take responsibility for your own heart. Take responsibility for your own actions and words. It begins with taking our thoughts captive and making them obedient to Christ, as it says in **2 Corinthians 10:5**. The enemy of our soul is gunning to destroy your relationship. God promises to provide everything you need to work through your differences. You have the power, through the Holy Spirit of the living God to take control. You are not subject to the enemy. The enemy is subject to Christ. You have to take the responsibility. How do you do that?

Before a thought becomes comfy in your heart, it comes through your head. You have a choice to accept those thoughts or reject those thoughts. I'm in charge, not my mouth. Seriously, God gives you the ability to control your tongue. It's a hard job, so He gives us His Spirit to help. I have to run my thoughts through a filter:

The Words Filter

T   - Is it true?

H   - Is it helpful?

I   - Is it inspiring?

N   - Is it necessary?

K   - Is it kind?

We must run our words through a filter BEFORE we say them. Is it true? Is it helpful? Is it inspiring? Is it necessary? Is it kind? Our words have to make it through all of those filters. Not just one or two. Something can be true and necessary, but never make it through the filter of helpful and inspiring. Something might be inspiring (to you) but never passes through the other filters before reaching your spouse or family member.

If you start using this filter, you may very well be shocked at how much of what you want to say tends to get stuck in the filter.

"We demolish arguments and every pretension that sets itself up against the knowledge of God, and we take captive every thought to make it obedient to Christ."
2 Corinthians 10:5 NIV

I wish I could tell you that this is an easy thing for me. My mouth can run like a racehorse, and I can easily end up spewing things that are hurtful. Just because a thought comes into your mind, doesn't mean you should say it.

2 Corinthians 10:5 gives us a great word picture of what to do with those words before they come out and cause damage. I have to choose to take those thoughts captive, and make them obedient to Christ. I can either accept them, if they align with the Word of God, or reject them if they do not. The responsibility is mine.

Some people need word pictures to understand this principle. Maybe you need to take your arm, reach up and grab a hold of that thought. If that helps you to stop long enough to run it through the filter, then DO THAT. Reach up, compare those thoughts with the truth of God's Word, and then either accept them, let them settle in your heart, or reject them if they do not. If you do that and they are contrary to what God's Word says, shut it down!!!! ***"Take captive every thought and make it obedient to Christ."***

Here's the thing. We don't do this alone. When Jesus was getting ready to leave this earth, He told His disciples that He would send His Holy Spirit to live IN them. Read *John 14*. Then and only then would they have the power and ability to do the things that He did. He promised them that the Spirit would remind them of the things He taught them. He said that HIS SPIRIT WOULD BE IN THEM. You, as a son or daughter of The King, have His Spirit IN you.

That same Spirit that resonates from the Spirit of God in the foundation of **THIS PYRAMID**, gives you that same power. Use the power and authority He has given you. You are His son or daughter. You have all the same ability to capture those thoughts and make them obedient to Christ. But YOU have to do it.

SO WHAT'S ALL THIS TALK ABOUT SUBMISSION

Ephesians chapter 5 talks about wives submitting to their husbands and husbands loving their wives. People get all kinds of snarky (short tempered and irritable) when we talk about submitting. I often tell couples that: **there isn't a woman on earth that wouldn't submit to a man that loved her as Christ loved the Church and gave Himself for her. She can trust that love. There isn't a man on earth that wouldn't love his wife when he knows she submits to his love as she does to Christ.**

Take special note in *Ephesians 5*, **before** the Apostle talks about wives submitting and husbands loving, he said this: *verse 21 in the NIV: "Submit to one another out of reverence for Christ."*

The *NLT* brings a little more clarity when it says, *"Be willing to help and care for each other because of Christ. By doing this, you honor Christ."*

That helps us take a different look at the word "submission," doesn't it? **It's not** (with a loud, demanding voice) "submit to what I say or else." It's being willing to **help and care for each other because of Christ.**

How do I speak and act toward my husband? How do you speak and act toward your husband or wife? Do we treat them the way Jesus treats us? Or do we treat them the way we think they deserve to be treated? Wait – what? Yes, you read that right. Do I treat him according to what he deserves, or do I treat him as Jesus treats me?

Jesus never gives me what I deserve. He gives me what I need. I need love, grace and mercy, and those are the very things He uses to draw me to Him. When I act the jerk, I deserve for Him to slap me upside my silly head. But does He do that? No, He uses His word to draw me to Him. He promises me that no matter how I am, He will never leave or forsake me. He will love me always. He gives me what I need, not what I deserve. Make no mistake about it. He will correct me, but He does it with love, grace and mercy. And it is that love, grace and mercy that draws me back to Him.

Even when we help our spouse see something that needs changing, it should be with that same love, grace and mercy because we want the blessing and favor of God on them AND on our marriage.

Ladies, he doesn't need you to be his mama. Guys, she doesn't need you to be her daddy either. You know what I'm talking about. If you're treating your spouse like a child, you need to stop it. I've done it. I'm well aware of how I can sound like his mama. I am his wife, his lover and friend. I'm not his mama. He will have little respect for me if I treat him like he's a child. The same is true for him. Respect for him will be hard if he treats me like a child.

THE CHOICES

We have choices every day on how we are going to treat our spouse. Will I give them what they need, or what they deserve? Will I give them love, grace and mercy, or will I give them judgment, criticism, tongue lashing or silent treatment?

We made a vow, to love and to cherish, in sickness and in health, for richer or for poorer, til death do us part. A vow doesn't include a choice to walk away. I took a pledge. We took a pledge. A big part of that pledge is that no matter what comes, we will work it through. We will do what it takes, with the Power of the Holy Spirit in **THIS PYRAMID**, to work it out. God promises that we don't walk it alone. He is the foundation. He will give us everything we need to work it out.

Pledges and vows don't mean as much to people today as they did in days of old. People walk away because the grass looks greener with someone else, or greener alone. Scripture tells us that it's better to not take one than to break one. We enter into a covenant relationship, man, woman and God. We often forget that piece.

Ecclesiastes 4:12 says: "A cord of three stands is not quickly broken." God will not break the covenant. The vow that we take says that we will not either.

The blessing and favor of God will never rest on you if you live outside the boundaries of His protection. He promises blessing and favor in our lives if we live according to His Word and the truths that are contained in it. He also promises blessing and favor when we take seriously the vows we took. If we choose to live according to our own standard of right and wrong, the blessing and favor of God will never fully be on us. We do what we must to find the path to a healthy and happy marriage. There are so many resources out there, and you know you have the greatest source INSIDE OF YOU.

TIME AND MOUNTAIN MOVING

Many times we become so impatient with the path of healing, whether it is physical, relational or any kind of problem we encounter. We expect everything to be solved quickly. Just like we expect drive-thru things in every other area of our lives, we expect that we should get instant help with relationships too. When it doesn't happen, we assume it is beyond fixing and want to move on.

We do indeed live in a day when you can get drive-thru anything: drive-thru food and prescriptions, drive-thru banking, weddings and prayer. Drive-thru and get what you need!!! *It has turned us in to very impatient people.* We expect God to give us what we need and we hang on to the promises with the expectation that we won't have to wait. And when we can't get it quick, we draw assumptions that either God failed, or He isn't real, or there's something wrong with the other person, or sin in our life, or...on and on and on. The real problem is that we have drive-thru mentality.

News flash — *sometimes God moves mountains one boulder at a time.* True! We don't like that, because we've grown so accustomed to everything being done **now**. I don't like that much, but it's true. It has proved true so many times in my life and I'm sure yours too, if you will be honest and think it through.

Something as simple as water bottles. I grew up in a time that nobody even thought of water bottles. Now, we take a bottle of water with us most every time we leave the house. At least I do. I remember being a kid in the car on a trip and lamenting to my Mom — "I'm so thirsty, I'm gonna die." Mom assured me that I would not die. When we get to our destination, surely there would be enough water to solve my thirst problem. If I didn't stop asking, she would say something profound like, "do you SEE a water faucet in this car?" Of course not! We learned to wait.

I'm really glad we now have water bottles. I really am. But now we have to make more stops to get rid of the water we consume in the car. Can't solve that at the drive-thru. Just saying.

COHABITATION BEFORE MARRIAGE

Another topic I hear a lot of today is regarding living together before marriage. It is so common and accepted in our society that we don't even flinch when we hear that a couple is living together. Even in the church, we've just learned to accept it as a social norm. Usually the reasons given are "purely economical." The very suggestion that it is against God's plan for His people is scoffed at and thought old fashion. The statistics regarding the decision to live together before marriage is astounding, but talked about very little. At the date of this writing, more than 50 percent of all people live together before marriage.

On the *Fireproof Your Marriage* website, Michael Foust addresses this issue very well and quotes Mike and Harriet McManus, authors of *Living Together: Myths, Risks, and Answers*. He said this:

Living Together: Myths, Risks, & Answers

"Men and woman cohabitate for different reasons," Mike McManus said in a conference call discussing the book. "Women see it as a step toward marriage. They think they can audition for this job. Men do it because they like to have the ready availability of sex and having someone share their living expenses. Women should heed their mother's advice − "if you give away the milk, he won't buy the cow."

Couples who live together not only are significantly more likely to divorce after marriage, but about 45 percent of them will break up before marriage, studies show.

Cohabitation, McManus said, has a high failure rate because it's based on selfishness. "If you make me feel loved, then I might marry you." "If you make me feel happy, then I might marry you."

"Love and marriage is an investment, and cohabitation is a gamble. *Cohabitation is conditional; marriage is based on permanence. These are radically different psychological premises. True love is selfless − seeking to serve the other person. Cohabitation is based on selfishness _ 'How will this relationship satisfy me?'"*

In looking at this issue in light of **THIS PYRAMID** and our **foundation**, if we build on **Christ and His Word**, we enter into a deep relationship with a desire to serve; a selfless, not selfish relationship. A love that runs so deep with a commitment to invest in this relationship "til death we do part." Marriage isn't a gamble. It's a commitment. Because marriage is a promise, a vow, it's based on serving, giving and love. It's not based on selfishness, and what I get.

For those reading that may have cohabitated before marriage, know this: if you have a love relationship with God, and the foundation of your relationship is solidly in Him, you do not have to be one of those statistics. You have the power of His Spirit IN you to live a life of blessing and the favor of God.

If you are cohabitating, I would strongly suggest you take steps to get this right. If I were counseling you, I would tell you that you need to separate for a time before you take your vows. Ask God's forgiveness for living in sin. When we ask Him, He forgives and remembers it no more. Start fresh, pure in heart and soul. God will bless you for it. His desire is to give you His blessing and favor for the rest of your lives. Don't let it pass you by.

THIS PYRAMID has a foundation that is solid. Listen to Him and His Word. Seek Him. Follow His path and begin looking at your spouse as the one you promised that you would serve. As we read – submitting to each other. Love rules. Love wins. He promises to give us everything we need in **THIS PYRAMID**.

A Little Lightening Up

I heard a true story – a couple was on their second marriage. Each had lost their first spouse through death. God brought them both together some time later, and they began their lives together as husband and wife.

One day, he got up, came downstairs to hear his wife say: "You know what day it is, right?" Now, the guys will know this kind of question can make a man freeze. So his quick response was, "I sure do." He put on his shoes and headed out the door. He came back a short time later with some flowers for her. She was delighted with the flowers, but then said, "This is the first time I ever got flowers for Groundhogs day."

They both had a good laugh. In some houses, that would have been said in a demeaning way, and he would have felt foolish and never tried to bless her again. Many couples treat each other in such demeaning ways. Lighten up! Learn to laugh WITH each other, not AT each other.

Your spouse is the love of your life. Or at least was at one point in time. Somewhere, it may have fallen off the track. Having a good marriage, having those feelings that I'm living with the love of my life doesn't mean that everything is AWESOME, that everything is perfect. But they are the person you took a vow for better or worse, in sickness or in health, for rich or poor, and til death do you part; the one that you committed to, and they to you.

Another silly story, but I'm pretty sure this is not true. This couple was standing before the minister, repeating their vows that went like this:

Minister:	for better or worse
Couple:	we'll take better
Minister:	richer or poorer
Couple:	we'll take richer
Minister:	sickness or in health
Couple:	we'll take health

Sorry, now I'm on a roll. **One more — after all, this section IS called "Lighten Up."**

Husband and wife were in the waiting room for the husband's doctor appointment. It wasn't long and the doc called the husband in for his examination.

After a complete exam, they both came out into the waiting room. The good doc asked the wife if she would come in, that he wanted to talk to her (this was before the HIPPA laws).

The doc said to the wife, "Well, here's the thing. What your husband needs to live out his days healthy and happy is for you to take care of all his needs. Cook all his favorite meals, bake his favorite treats, take care of his laundry and do all the shopping, make sure the house stays clean. Make sure he has everything he wants. Oh, and make sure he has as much sex as he wants."

The wife was a bit taken back, and said, "What if I don't do all that?" The good doc said, "Well, if you don't, your husband will surely die an early death."

They bid their farewells to the doc, and headed back to the car. After they got in the car, he asked his wife what the doc said to her. Without even a glance she said, "He said you're gonna die."

Sorry. No I'm not. Who am I kidding? That's hilarious.

UNBELIEVING SPOUSE

Before I go any further, I want to address the spouse that has an unbelieving other half. If just one of you is a believer, God will use you in some way to show the love of Christ to your spouse, or family members. If you refuse to allow God to use you, the breakdown will continue, and God's plan for marriage and family will not be realized in this or the next generation.

2 Corinthians 7:14 talks about how an unbelieving husband is "set apart" or "sanctified" by the believing wife. And an unbelieving wife is "set apart" or "sanctified" by the believing husband. God is working in your marriage and in the life of your spouse because of your faithfulness.

God will continue to bless your family because of who HE is, the God that loves your family more than you do. Believe it. He loves your spouse and your kids even more than you do. He sent His son to die for them. Continue to trust that and He will do amazing things. Fight for the souls of your spouse and your children. That, dear one, is your responsibility. Fight, in prayer, for the souls of your family.

FIGHT FOR YOUR FAMILY

I just read a book written by Nicky Cruz called *One Holy Fire.* God has anointed Nicky with an evangelistic calling. I never tire of experiencing crusades with Nicky Cruz. This past summer, we had the honor of working with Nicky Cruz Outreach, and their TRUCE initiative. TRUCE is an acronym that means: To Reach Urban Communities Everywhere. We were blessed to have Nicky and his wife Gloria here for a time, as well as much time personally spent with their daughter Alicia and her husband Patrick. They are wonderful people devoted to winning souls for Christ and loving people into the Kingdom of God. A true example of God's blessing and favor on a family that has a solid foundation on Christ.

In Nicky's book, he talks about the breakdown of the family. He is incredibly insightful in diagnosing the problems in our nation today in the chapter entitled *"The Battle for the Family."* In looking at what has changed in our society over the years, Nicky said this: "They (parents) allowed their kids to grow up too quickly and weren't there to guide them and teach them right from wrong. In an effort to give their children material goods, fathers worked harder and longer hours. Mothers flocked to the workplace during a time when their children needed them most. Kids were left to fend for themselves, and today we're experiencing the consequences of our misguided decisions."

About the misguided decisions, the drug problems and violence, Nicky went on to say: **"It was obvious then that the real cause of this addictive and destructive behavior was not poverty, but the breakdown of the family unit."**

We have done this. I am from Milwaukee, WI. I love my town. I was born and raised in this, once called, blue-collar town. Not long ago, there was big trouble in our city. Our city, in fact, has a long history of racial and economic divides. My city is broken. Recently, another young black man was killed on our streets and the burning of buildings ensued as violence took to the streets with a voice that needed to be heard. The problem ISN'T POVERTY! The problem is the breakdown of the family.

It is truly a complicated issue, and one that I am not prepared to fully address right now, nor do I claim to know all of the issues and solutions. I did feel, however, it needed to be brought out at this point in THIS layer of **THIS PYRAMID** because we're talking about families. We are seeing all around us single parent homes and babies having babies. Young people that struggle with finding a good path, mostly because they don't have good role models.

Even as Christian families, we are seeing the same breakdown. This is a HUGE difficult topic. Even in the family of God, those that say their foundation is on Christ, we are seeing monumental breakdowns. All of the same problems that occur in secular homes are being seen in Christian homes. One could say with a measure of certainty that "the enemy is gunning for the kids." And they would be accurate. Isn't it our responsibility to fight for the souls of our families? If we continue to blame everyone and everything, who will fight for the souls of our families?

During a Revival Service in the summer of 2016, I heard the **Rev. Tony Whitley** speak about **"Taking Back the Streets."** He said this: **"if we are going to talk about taking back our streets, then we have to assume that we once had them."** That statement pierced my heart. If we once had them, what was going on when we did? How did we lose them? He was articulate in sharing what it was like when we had them. How we were all accountable to each other. In how we were all willing to take responsibility for not only our own kids, but all the kids in the neighborhood.

As Mother Theresa said: "If you want to change the world, go home and love your family." Safe to say we have abandoned our families when we abandon our marriages. Families are suffering from a great divide. Please know I do NOT intend to heap guilt on anyone. We are where we are. We start where we are. ***It's time though, that we begin fighting for our marriages. It's time though, that we begin fighting for our families.***

It is our responsibility to fight for their souls. Here's the breakdown. Marriages get in trouble and we don't even know it until someone is ready to walk out the door and divorce. Pastoring for many years, I know that we don't often know a marriage is in trouble until it's "crash and burn" time. They walk in my door and I know before anyone even sits down what the conversation is going to be like.

I've had couples in the office come in scraping with each other and yet others are silent. Minds made up and they're just done. Often, one spouse wants to be there and the other does not. There are glazed looks by the one that has already made up their mind that it's done, and crushing pain in the other, who wants some resolve and to do the hard work to be faithful to their vows.

> *If you want to change the world, go home and love your family.*
>
> *Mother Theresa*

Not a Win for the Kids

The world has sold us, yes, us in the church, that divorce is a win for the kids. No it's not. It's NOT a win for the kids. It's a win for the ones that want to do their own thing and they don't mind the consequences to their kids. They've bought a hill of goods that it's just better for "us." You must know this, most young children will feel that your divorce is their fault. No matter what you tell them, they will think it was their fault. They will also spend their young lives believing and hoping that you will get back together again. Like it or not, it's true.

Now, please know that I realize that there are just some difficult things that cause people to head for divorce.

Anyone that has worked with abuse issues knows that there are some that need to move on because of abuse in their home. They MUST protect their children. I'm not talking about them. My heart aches for them. My heart breaks for the breakdown in morals. I believe the heart of God aches more than I ever could at seeing people with the upside down theology they use as an excuse for their abusive behavior. They excuse themselves and make it all sound so necessary. It's not those victims of abuse that I'm talking about. I understand and I believe God does too.

It's the many others who just decide, "it's just too hard." "I just don't love them anymore." "God wants me to be happy, and I'm just not happy any more." Some convince themselves AND their kids that, "we're just not good together."

Then we hear of yet others that find all kinds of so called, "good reasons", and find out later that there was someone in the wings waiting for them. So we don't call it adultery, we find other reasons to justify our walking away, when it really has to do with finding another, and forsaking their wedding vows.

Yikes. What a mess we're in. As Christians we need to wake up. When our foundation is built on Christ, we seek Him when things are tough. Tough things happen in marriage. I understand that. We just celebrated 47 years of marriage. I can't applaud us. I can, however, applaud our God who has helped us when things went goofy. There were plenty of times when one of us did some pretty stupid stuff. But at the end of the day, we made a decision to work it through. At the end of the day, we knew it was the enemy of our soul that wanted to destroy our marriage, and blow up our family. We decided we would not risk our family being blown up.

There were times in our lives when one turned to God and the other did not. Or times when the "voice of God" was mistaken or misunderstood and it nearly tore us apart. But God! But God!!! Because of Him, we stand together and we are honored to be used by Him in marriage ministry. Not because we got it all together. But rather it's because we've done so many dumb things that we learned the hard way. We messed up pretty bad. But because of all that God has done IN us, we turn all glory and praise to Him.

We MUST take responsibility for our marriages.
We MUST take responsibility for our families.
<u>**Their souls are at stake.**</u>

There are many great churches that realize the breakdown of the family and do everything they can to reach out to couples. Kudos to those ministries! Even though couples struggle, they find God's path for a healthy marriage, submit to each other and continue to serve Him and lead their families to do the same. Marriages thrive when we feed them. But even in the best environment, there will be some that cross the great divide and decide it's not worth the effort. That not only breaks my heart, but every church leader I know, grieves the loss of even one marriage in their congregation.

The Triangle Principle

I've heard some couples say that their marriages are of prime importance, but do their best to separate God from their marriage. The foundation of a good marriage is found in Christ. If that relationship is good, the next level will be a reflection of that.

There's a triangle principle that many people have used for years. It's really simple, yet so complex as we try to walk it out day after day. The closer the husband and wife draw to God, the closer they become to each other. It's a Godly principal. Simple!

Trust Your Training and Your Partner

I recently spoke at a women's conference on Limitless Courage. In preparing for this message, I did some research by interviewing professionals like Law Enforcement, Firefighters, Medical Professionals and Educators in difficult assignments.

One of the things that stood out in every one of them was this: they learned to trust their training and trust in those on their teams. They support each other, work together and lives are saved. People in crisis situations who needed the help of any one of those professionals could rest assured that their team was working together.

There's no fighting in the field about what's the right thing to do. The stakes are too high. There's a chain of command, and they trust that chain of command. They may have discussions AFTER the fact, mostly for clarification and understanding. To challenge each other is unthinkable, and it can cost not only their job, but other lives that are at stake.

I see too many couples fight against each other, like the other is the enemy. If your foundation is on Christ, if you've built **THIS PYRAMID** the way it was designed, you're on the same team. You must learn to trust your partner. Ladies, trust him. Guys, trust her. God has hard wired us each so different. You need to be ok with that. We are God's design and we each have strengths and weaknesses that we support in each other, not fight against each other.

We live in a world today that speaks of inclusiveness. Somehow, we don't know how to do that with marriage. We think if they were "just like me", life would be good. No it wouldn't. You'd either kill each other or never get anything done. God put you together because you need each other, strengths/weaknesses; warts, pimples, good, bad and ugly. You are a team. We just need to learn how to walk that out in every day life.

LAURIE GANIERE

Men and Respect

Dr. Emerson Eggerichs wrote an amazing book called *Love and Respect*. The principles in this book are timeless. I hear couples who say often, "Why didn't someone teach us this stuff when we first got married. This makes so much sense." Yes it does. If you have not read the book, you need to pick up a copy ASAP.

There are a couple of concepts we have learned over the last 47 years that we have found amazingly helpful. You don't get to be married this long without learning a lot of things the hard way. It's amazing that we are still together. Only because **THIS PYRAMID** is built on a firm foundation, are we standing here together today.

God has created every man with a need for respect. Like it or not, God has hard wired men to need respect. Because there is such a deep need for respect, his **greatest fear is that of failure.** If he feels he's going to fail at something, he'll do one of two things: either he'll work himself to death trying to get it right, or he'll give up on it because it's too much trouble to fight the fear of failure.

That gives wives a couple choices regarding his fear of failure. We can throw water on it, or we can throw gasoline on it. Water will douse that fear, but gasoline will cause it to erupt into a forest fire. And the choice is mine which container I pick up: the water jug or the gasoline can.

A quick example of that principle: Rick was working on something for me and it didn't turn out the way he

84

thought. Seriously, that's unusual because he's talented, driven and very capable of doing most anything. If he doesn't know how to do something, he'll work hard to figure it out.

So when he made a mistake with this one thing, his comment, out of sheer frustration, was: "How stupid can I be." Wait, what? Stupid? This man is far from stupid. But, none the less, I had two choices: pick up the jug of water or the can of gasoline.

Gasoline would have said: "Yeah, what the heck were you thinking. That **was** pretty stupid. You know better." That, or any form of that, would ignite the fire of failure in his soul.

But to douse the fire of failure is to throw water on it: "You are far from stupid. You simply made a mistake. No big deal. You'll fix it." Any variation of that approach will douse the flames of failure and encourage him to move on. And reassure him of my love and belief in him as a man, and as my husband.

Women and Love

Now guys, your lady's greatest need is to feel and be treasured, and because of that, her greatest fear is insecurity.

How would you treat something that you treasure? Well, I would say you guard it, and you protect it. You make sure it's always safe or in a protected place.

Because of her deep need to be treasured it makes sense then that her greatest fear is that feeling of insecurity. I said in the first section that her security is found in Christ. And it is! But as her husband, there is a certain level of security that she will look to you to provide. You can either feed that insecurity or starve it. You can either throw gasoline on it and cause a forest fire in her soul where it appears that everything is falling down around her, or you can douse it with water and reassure her that all is well.

And you must do it in a loving, caring way, not a condescending kind of way. If you are condescending, she'll know it and think you just have your head in the sand. If she feels insecure, she will more than likely decide that you're not there for her, and that she has to fix it herself. You have the ability to help her feel secure in the midst of the challenge. Reassurance is the greatest thing you can do for her.

Whatever you do, don't tell her, "You shouldn't feel that way." Seriously!!! She feels what she feels, and it does absolutely nothing to tell her that she shouldn't feel. Feelings just are.

SCENERIO: I remember when I left my full-time position at a wonderful church. I knew it was God moving me on. It was a great church and I loved the people and the ministry that God allowed me to be a part of, but walking away left me feeling a great loss. God helped me navigate through that well, and He used my husband Rick to help. Interestingly, Rick, who hates change, was the one that God used to help me navigate that change. He helped me see that I was of value, not just what I did. God has hard wired me to help people. When I was out of that environment where I did that every day, I felt insecure in **who** I was in Christ. Rick gave me the space I needed to find a new normal and helped me to learn to enjoy the journey. That was hard for me. A lot of my value is in what I do. It helps me to feel treasured.

If he had grabbed the gasoline can, he would have caused a fire that would have left me feeling insecure in God and in him. He could have easily belittled me and told me to get over it and move on. He could have spoken words that would feed my fear, my insecurity. Instead, he grabbed the water jug and helped me realize just how treasured I was. He also reassured me that God would show me what I needed and when. And He did. Rick could have said something foolish like, "Why are you all wrapped up in yourself? Can't you see life isn't just about how you feel?" But, he did not. He treasures me, and because he does, he never picks up the gas can.

I encourage you to invest in your spouse. Invest in your family. Knowing the love (treasured) and respect thing should be a BIG deal with your family. If you have kids, you need to help them understand this principle.

We have a grave responsibility to allow the light of the Holy Spirit to shine up through **THIS PYRAMID**, into the lives of everyone in our family. The cost to not get this right is too great. The cost is their souls.

Holy Spirit shine through **THIS PYRAMID**, yours and mine.

I highly recommend a couple of good resources for marriage. The first one is Marriage Encounter. It is for marriages that need a boost, and they do a wonderful job of drawing couples closer to each other and to God. You can find their website at www.agme.org. The cost is very affordable and truly a weekend to invest in your marriage.

There are also couples who are in major crisis and don't know what to do, or where to turn. I strongly recommend Marriage Restored. I have sent numerous couples through the years to a Marriage Restored weekend, many of them ready for divorce, and they have come back refreshed, with a new vision for their marriage, for each other, and their God. Their website is: www.marriagerestored.com.

At our Marriage Matters seminars, we give away many resources. Some of them are books by wonderful men and women that are dedicated to seeing marriages not just succeed, but flourish and find paths to fulfillment in the grind of daily life. Some of those authors are: Jimmy Evans, Gary Thomas, Ted Cunningham, Craig and Amy Groeschel, Dr. Emerson Eggerichs, Les and Leslie Parrott, Gary Chapman, Drs. Cloud and Townsend, and so many more. I know when we start listing names, there are always some wonderful authors and speakers that get left out. Please know this is not a comprehensive list.

ABUSE, DIVORCE AND DEATH

Abuse

If there is abuse in your past, or even in your present, I want you to know that God loves you and your abuse was NEVER a part of His plan and purpose for you. NEVER. So many have asked me, "Pastor Laurie, if God is a good God, why didn't He stop my abuse?" That question can stop even the best Pastor in their tracks, just because it's so hard to answer. But you must know that God loves you.

God has given every human being the right to choose to follow Him or choose to live their lives to satisfy their sinful, lustful flesh. We all have freedom of choice. Your abuser, even if they proclaim to be a Christian (God forbid), has that choice. Abuse at any time, in any form is a horrific crime against another human being. In the life of the abuser, it is sin that has its root in sinful flesh, and desire to please themselves no matter the cost to another. Sadly, they make up most any reason to make it ok. They will even blame the victim to avoid taking responsibility. It is NEVER ok. It WAS never ok.

In the course of eight or nine years, I worked with over one hundred women that have been abused in some way: sexual, emotional, verbal, physical and even economic abuse. Many of them have felt that for one reason or another, they were responsible for their abuse. Many sat in my office and wept when they realized their innocence. There were a few of them, women in their 50's, that were totally convinced that their rape was their fault. They were in their early teens, and were certain that what happened to them, rape and incest, was their fault. Or others that had such horrible verbal and physical abuse that seriously thought that "if I only acted better, he wouldn't have gotten so mad." Or "if I would have answered her different, she wouldn't have thrown me against the wall and locked me in the closet." "If only I would have..."

No one abuse is worse than another. Abuse is abuse. My heart used to ache working with the classes of those that have been hurt so desperately. My husband knew the pain of some of those weeks in the classroom. He would pray especially for "my girls", as I walked out of the house to go meet with them. They were "my girls", entrusted to me by my Father to help put on the healing balm of the Holy Spirit, the one and only Healer. There's nothing special about me. This wasn't about me. It was about God giving His daughters a chance to learn truth, and find freedom in Him.

When I remind these precious souls, those that thought it was their fault, that there are laws to protect children, it's like an epiphany happens right there in the office or classroom. When they realize that they were only twelve, or only thirteen, or only five or six, or you name the age of the child, and not responsible for the atrocities done to them, there comes a point when a light goes on. It is only then that true healing can begin. Some have said, "No you don't understand. If I hadn't been there," or "if I wasn't a girl," or "if I wasn't in a dress," or " if I only didn't say anything," or...you name it. My statement usually is something like "Sweetheart, listen to me. That is why there are laws to protect children. You were a child. You could not protect yourself. You couldn't have done anything. Abuse is a sin that is bound in the heart of a man or woman and God HATES it."

Know this, God was screaming in the ear of your abuser to stop, and they refused to listen to God.

If you have suffered abuse, you would do well to seek out someone who can help you find a path of health and healing. If you don't, there are cycles in your life that will repeat themselves through your adult life. A good pastor or counselor will recognize those cycles and be able to refer you to someone trustworthy to help.

You deserve better, and God wants and has healing for you. If you are a woman, you would be well served to have another woman help you. If you are a guy, it needs to be another guy. The issues are far too sensitive.

One of the resources that I have used for many years is written by my friend, pastor and author, **Gwen Tackett**. She wrote a study guide called **Vessels of Honor.** It is a wonderful curriculum to walk through with someone you trust, and will help you find help, hope and healing from the abuses you've lived through. I strongly urge you to order the book, and find a trusted pastor or Godly friend to walk the journey of **Vessels** with you.

Pastor Gwen and her husband, Pastor Arnold, have written the book in a way that can help for couples to go through together. She was a victim, and together they wrote this curriculum to help others. You can order the book at www.nameonline.net. Go to their store and you will find it there. I promise, you won't be sorry.

Those that Are Divorced

Before I get too far into this, I must say this: some of you are divorced. I know that because the statistics tell us that a huge percentage of our society is divorced. Some of you have been married and divorced more than once. The last thing I want to do is cause harm by inflicting guilt and shame on you if you have walked that path that led to divorce. Some of you struggle daily, while others are just so relieved the nightmare is over. In **THIS PYRAMID**, the light of the Holy Spirit of God shines in and on you. His love for you is so deep, so intimate. The aftermath of divorce can make us feel like His love is far from us. Dear one, know this, He loves you. He loves your children. He loves your former spouse.

Protect your children. The blessing and favor of God will continue to be on you as you protect your children from the details of the divorce.

So please know I do not intended to shame you or make you feel like a leper in the Christian world. People divorce for a lot of reasons. Some very good reasons, while others pretty lame and self-serving. Regardless of where you are today, God loves you and has a plan for you moving forward. As Billy Graham once said, "you can't unscramble eggs." What is, is, and we move on in the grace, mercy and love of an awesome God. If you don't have anyone walking with you on this journey as a single or single parent, I urge you to seek a Godly mentor, or prayer group. Be cautious of future relationships. Seek God, His direction and will for your future. Evangelistic dating is not wise. Entering in to a spiritually unbalanced relationship will only lead down a path without the blessing and favor of God. Be cautious and wait for God. His best is what you want.

One great resource for those who are divorced is a program called Divorce Care. This is a national ministry that has been such a blessing to so many. If you still struggle with the affects of divorce, go to their website www.divorcecare.org and find a group near you.

Death of a Spouse

I don't want to miss those that may have suffered the death of a spouse. There's no time frame with grief. God loves you. He has not forgotten you. The pain of loss of the person closest to you is unimaginable! I remember when my dad died. A piece of my mom died that day. She was a Christian. She knew Jesus was there with her. But the pain of that grief is beyond belief. I only wish there was a Griefshare program around for mom then. They too, are a national ministry and led by some of the most compassionate, loving people I've ever met. Go to their website, www.griefshare.org, find a group, and get there. If going alone is too hard, ask a friend or family member to go with you.

After my dad's death, a suicide death, I saw an add in the paper for a group at a local Memorial Park for people that lost a loved one to suicide. My Aunt Lois went with me. I was forever grateful for her, as going alone was more than I could bear. If you are in that place, find someone to go with you. If you know of someone that lost a loved one, offer to go with them. You will never regret investing in their lives.

LAURIE GANIERE

PART THREE
The Penguin Principles

LAURIE GANIERE

The third level in **THIS PYRAMID** is with church family and others that we are close with on a regular basis. One thing I've learned over my many years of life is that those that we are the closest to, we tend to hurt more often. We become insensitive and just figure they should understand the rules of relationship and certainly they should know better. In the church, we often times expect more from each other and set the bar of expectations pretty high. When people don't meet "our" expectations, we get critical and question their spirituality. How dare we!

If we are honest, we accept that people are just people. Because we are living, learning, and doing life together, it requires patience, grace and mercy, every day.

So, tell me, why the title, "The Penguin Principles?"

I was inspiried by the movie, *March of the Penguins,* in 2005 on a flight from Milwaukee, WI to Quepos, Costa Rica, to do missions work. I was so inspired by the purpose and instincts of those penguins. They are so determined to accomplish their purpose, that little to nothing could stop them. I saw some correlations between those penguins and humans in relationship to each other.

After nearly a week of working hard with those beautiful Costa Rican people and our team of 20, we had a day to spend at the beach. Some had gone zip lining, and others spent time sunning and frolicking in the incredible waves of the ocean. While on the beach, I saw some

99

principles from those penguins and how they could apply to us as humans, and particularly as Christians.

Several of us chose to spend our free day at the ocean. The waves were huge and absolutely awesome to ride. What we didn't know is that one of our team members could not swim. It was impossible for her to stay on her feet when the waves rolled in. They came in with such a force that the sand disappeared from under her feet, and under the water she would go. The sheer force of the waves made it impossible for her to navigate and not be taken to the depths of the ocean. When we realized the trouble she was in, we all came close to grab her before the waves rushed in. After we were sure she was safe, we laughed like crazy, knowing we had survived another wave.

In the movie, during the storms of the arctic, the penguins stood close together to protect the whole group. No one was more important than another. They stood together to protect each other. Together, with their bodies pulled tight together forming a big circle, creating safety for all, even the weakest of them from the ravages of winter. As you can imagine, the ones in the middle of the circle stayed the warmest. To keep everyone warm, they ever so slowly rotated through the circle, so that every one of them had a chance at the warmer, center parts of the circle. They were able to withstand the horrible storm as they stayed close together, keeping each other warm.

As we continued to enjoy the ocean, we would yell out with loud voices "Penguin", when we saw another huge wave, and we all quickly assembled to help her take the wave. We reminisced how in the *March of the Penguins* they all look out for each other and pull together to keep each safe and warm. In a strange way, we became like those penguins. We would lock arms, stand together in a tight circle, and we all were safe; wet and battered, but all good. The weakest no longer had to worry. We were a team, whether we were building classrooms for this church in Costa Rica, doing children's ministries back in the remote areas of the country, or standing in the waves of the ocean.

That was back in 2005. The majority of the mission's team to Costa Rica were from the Singles Group that I pastored. I was so inspired by those penguins in that movie that I developed a three-week class called "Penguin Principles" for our Wednesday night Bible Study.

Fast forward, seven years. I went into semi-retirement, ready to launch a new ministry with my husband. My life was full of deep emotion. I was leaving a wonderful church and staff where I had been an associate pastor for twelve years. We had developed beautiful relationships with some pretty awesome people at that church. To say it was hard to leave is an understatement. As my office was packed up and I was unloading all my books, files and memorabilia into my home office, God spoke to me and said, "What about the Penguin Principles? Didn't I tell you I wanted you to write about them? Now is your time to write."

My prayer is that you are able to glean something from these principles and apply them to your life as well as apply to those that you love and serve.

PRINCIPLE 1 - CHURCH FAMILY AND OTHER CLOSE RELATIONSHIPS

How is it that in life, we try to do so much on our own? Some of us are more independent than others and really have trouble looking to others for help to accomplish things in life. We take great pride in just being able to do it ourselves. God did not create us to do life alone. As we have seen in the first two parts of **THIS PYRAMID**, God created us for relationship: first of all with Him, and secondly with others. Remember, **THIS PYRAMID** has the Holy Spirit coming forth through every relationship, from the foundation, our relationship with Christ.

Everything is foundational to that – God calls us to relationship with Him. He has a plan for our lives, individually and corporately. Throughout His Word, we see clearly how we can live together in unity, in love, and locking arms together that the world would see Him though us. Like generations that have gone on before us though, we struggle with living well in community. We like the idea of living well together, but it's just hard to do. Often we do for a short time, until something comes between us, or someone offends us, or we just decide it's easier to do it alone.

Someone once said that doing life together as Christians is kind of like living with porcupines. We do fine together until we get too close. We don't like it much when we start getting poked by the sharp quills that come from getting to know someone. Previous learning has told us that those quills are for predators, to keep the porcupine safe. I quickly deduce that if I'm getting poked, they must see me as a predator. I'm no predator, so I'm outta here. I would ask you to begin thinking about living with penguins, rather than porcupines. Way cuter, and so much more productive, in my opinion. Using the principles in **THIS PYRAMID**, it is imperative that we look at doing life together a little differently. It's true, time is short and eternity is long. We need to make every relationship count for eternity.

I've seen so many people hurt by church people over the years, and I'm sure I've hurt my fair share. It saddens me that we can say and do such hurtful things when we are, in fact, supposed to be the hands and feet of Jesus to those in our sphere of influence. I'm ashamed to think about the times I may have been the offender, and it was my sharp quills that caused someone else to decide that church life isn't for them. I've asked God to forgive me, as well as to touch those I may have offended over the years, and repair any damage I may have caused.

During outreach events, I have often picked up a microphone and asked those in attendance for forgiveness for anything that a Christian or Church may have caused them in the past. I ask them to please forgive us for the hurt that may have been inflicted on them or their families.

It's amazing to me how people soften when they feel like someone really cares enough to acknowledge that they might have been treated like jerks by someone else calling themselves Christian. It moves a mountain for many of them. The love of Christ covers a multitude of sins. It may take some time to prove to others that we won't do the same to them, but it is an investment that we must make if we are to be the true Church. There are mountains in the lives of others that will move, even if it is one boulder at a time. If we want to reflect the Spirit of a Living God that gave His life for others, then His light must shine through us, through **THIS PYRAMID** of relationships in our sphere of influence. This is an investment into the lives of others that is crucial.

So what about the times when we, as Christians, are hurt by others in the church? The Holy Spirit often reminds me that if my eyes are on myself and not on Christ, I will take offense at the smallest things. Enough of those small offenses and I can draw conclusions that Christians are just fake, unforgiving, unloving, or whatever is the most current hurt.

> *If we want to reflect the Spirit of a Living God that gave His life for others, then His light must shine through us, through THIS PYRAMID of relationships in our sphere of influence.*

When my eyes are on me, I take everything personal. I can't shake it off because I am so inwardly focused. If I find my sustenance in my relationship with Christ, I won't be hurt so badly by others and I will see the great need to be a part of the Church. This is way bigger than me.

Most of us know what it's like to be a part of a family. Some families are healthy and some are terribly unhealthy. As I said earlier in the book, I firmly believe that most every family has some level of dysfunction; it is just a matter of how much. Some people live in their own funk for so long that they don't even know how funky it is. It takes the light of the Holy Spirit to enter into that mess and clean up that funk. You and I should be that light in every relationship in our life. Not to clean someone up, but to show the love of Christ. They must understand that HE walks with them on the journey toward wholeness. Our job is to reflect the image of the God that loves them.

As a family, the Body of Christ, we can have our own dysfunction. Because it's ours, we think it's normal. We have to get this right family! Our dysfunction as a body has the ability to push people away from Christ rather than draw them TO Him. Time is too short, and many lives are at stake. Jesus is coming soon and there simply is too much work to do. There are too many souls that are lost and need to know Jesus.

In calling ourselves "the Church", one question we must ask is this: Does my life portray the biblical definition of the church, or do I still have the stench of the world all over me? We just need to look at how we portray Christ. **THIS PYRAMID** can never be what God calls it to be if we have the stench of the world all over us.

If we truly believe that when we enter into relationship with Jesus, and His Holy Spirit comes in us to dwell, it will change the way we live. The things we used to enjoy doing, we don't enjoy as much any more.

I remember so clearly looking at Christians and wondering if they had any fun. My interpretation of fun back then included all kinds of things that we ingested and partook in some dangerous activities. I had no idea that when the Holy Spirit came IN me that my life would get more exciting than I could ever imagine. Life in Jesus changes the way we live. I have more fun now than any other time in my whole life.

If Jesus changes the way we live, how is that experienced in community? How is that experienced in the Church? How does it reflect the Holy Spirit in

THIS PYRAMID? It reflects in every relationship in our life! Period! It changes the way we approach and treat those who are close, and even those in community. The penguins teach a lot about that.

One thing I saw so clearly in those penguins, is that:

- Instinctively they know that **they need each other**.
- They **depend on each other**.
- They **fight for each other** and keep each other's kids safe from predators.
- They **go without so that their kids can survive**, and survive well.
- Some take care of the family, while others travel thousands of miles in search of food for the family.
- They truly **band together during storms** and instinctively know to protect each other.
- They have to **work together**.

I see so many parallels that we as the body of Christ simply need to be reminded of or taught. How do we treat each other? I think there's a lot to learn from our little penguin friends.

We live in such a "drive-thru" culture today, we barely know people well enough to treat each other with such care as those penguins.

Regardless of who you are, and what size church you attend, the principles of **THIS PYRAMID** will carry the light of the Holy Spirit to everyone. The Bible mandates us as His people to have the light of Christ shining through every relationship: close, casual or acquaintances. We would do just what those penguins did: take care of each other, depend on each other, fight for each other, and in storms band together so all would be safe. And lastly work together. Then the light of the Spirit would shine through every layer of **THIS PYRAMID**.

So, instinct. Let's talk about it!

PRINCIPLE 2 - INSTINCT

In the movie, **March of the Penguins**, Morgan Freeman said that penguins instinct is like "an invisible compass." They just know where to go. They just know what to do. *"Their destination is always the same, but the terrain is not."* They just know. That's instinct.

A dictionary.com definition of instinct is:
- an inborn pattern of activity or tendency to action common to a given biological species
- a natural or innate impulse, inclination or tendency
- a natural aptitude or gift
- natural intuitive power

The question I would ask is this: Is there such a thing as instinct in the life of a Christian?

I have talked to others asking that exact question. "Is there something inside of us as Christians that just knows how to respond to something going on outside of us?" The discussions were fascinating. Some people were really puzzled by the question, didn't know how to answer. Others, clearly thinking about the power of the Holy Spirit in the life of a believer, had fun discussing all that it meant to have the Holy Spirit as our "instinct".

Luke 12:12 NIV "the Holy Spirit will teach you at that time what you should say."

John 16:13 NIV "But when he, the Spirit of truth, comes, he will guide you into all truth. He will not speak on his own; he will speak only what he hears, and he will tell you what is yet to come."

The incredible Spirit of God lives inside each and every believer, giving the truth, giving us words to say when we have none, telling us what to say, where to go and when. We have the choice every day to decide if we want to follow what that Spirit tells us or ignore His voice.

Some people are so puzzled about how to hear the voice of God. Most often God's voice comes through time in His Word, the Bible. Other times it's through time spent in prayer. Yet other times it is the voice of a friend, a song on the radio, a message preached in service. Deep in the heart of every Christian is the desire to really hear Him. At the end of the day, it's a deep knowing, confirmed through His Word, prayer and time spent with Him. It's as good as our knower can know. That is the Holy Spirit leading us, guiding us, directing us, and giving us words.

Just a side note: I once heard it said that a voice of a friend, circumstances, songs and such things will confirm His Will or direction, not create it.

Crowding Out the Spirit

Day to day life tends to crowd out the voice of the Spirit. That is why it is of primary importance for the Christ follower to maintain a close relationship with Him through the Word of God, communication with Him in prayer, and in worship. The highest form of worship to our God is an obedient life. We can't please Him without obedience. We can't be doing ungodly things and still expect to hear His voice. God will never tell you to do something that doesn't align with His Word.

1 Samuel 15:22 NLT "But Samuel replied, "What is more pleasing to the Lord: your burnt offerings and sacrifices or your obedience to his voice? Listen! Obedience is better than sacrifice, and submission is better than offering the fat of rams."

We don't sacrifice rams any more in this culture, but we allow ourselves to be so busy with doing things FOR God, that we miss the main things He tells us to do. Those things can crowd out the voice of the Spirit.

There's a story about a dad and his son that is a perfect example of what I mean. One day dad and mom had to leave the house to run some errands. The dad said to his son, "Son, while your mother and I are gone, get your room cleaned. Pick up everything and put it away, make your bed and run the vacuum." Sounds pretty detailed, not much room for misunderstanding right?

Son says, "OK dad, no prob." A couple hours later the dad and mom return and the son runs to meet them in the driveway all excited, big smile on his face and says, "Hey dad, hey mom." They all walk in to the house and everything looks awesome. The dad says, "So what did you get done while I was gone?"

The son, pretty proud of himself, said, "Well dad, I cleaned up the dishes and put them away. Then I cleaned up the living room and vacuumed. Then I even went into the bathroom and cleaned the tub after I took a bath." The dad says, "but did you clean your room like I asked?" "Naw," said the son, "I'll get to that later."

The dad was not pleased. Even though all the things the son did were great, they were not the things the dad asked of him. It's easier than we think to do that which seems right and not do THE right thing. Is your relationship with God resulting in your obedience to doing what He has asked of you, or are you just busy doing stuff that seems right in your own eyes, and leaving that other thing until later? It's easier than you think to get caught in that cycle. *Partial or delayed obedience is really disobedience.* There have been times in my life that I did that very thing. I wonder, can you see yourself in that place too? This will crowd out the voice of the Spirit.

Why am I talking about obedience right now? Weren't we talking about the penguins and instinct? Yes, we were. Still are. The problem with disobedience is it messes with your instinct. You start doing what seems right to you, and it has little to nothing to do with what God wants.

The Apostle Paul says in *2 Corinthians 10:12 NIV* *"...when they measure themselves by themselves and compare themselves with themselves, they are not wise."* How easy it is to do what we think is right and completely walk in disobedience to Him, even when trying to do good. We willy nilly walk through seasons of life doing good things, but not THE things He's called us to do. Seriously, it's easier than you think. The little boy did wonderful things. Who wouldn't like to come home to a house that is all cleaned up? But the boy missed it. I'm sure he was very disappointed that his dad was not pleased. I'm also pretty sure this was a great teaching moment for the dad and his son. The spiritual application is pretty obvious about obedience and how we get caught up in doing good. Just as Samuel said, "obedience is better than sacrifice."

Our Father wants to bless us. Blessing follows obedience. I wonder how often we miss the blessing because we focused on another thing. We sacrificed the lesser and missed the blessing of the best. We totally miss it! We ignore that instinct that draws us to obedience, with blessing to follow.

God is not a dictator, He gives us a choice to listen to Him or not. He loves us enough that He places His Holy Spirit IN us. He makes it easy, yet we can choose to not listen. Until the day we meet Him face to face, we have that same choice. He desires that we live IN Him, and live in the blessing and favor of living IN Him. But the choice is ours.

The Inner Compass and GPS

I have a car with a compass in the mirror. That compass will tell me clearly which direction I'm headed. It can't MAKE me go a different direction, but it will show me the direction I'm headed. In the same way, the Holy Spirit will show us if we're going the right direction or not. God loved us too much to expect us to hopefully find the path. His Holy Spirit leads, guides, directs, and lets us know when we're on course and when we're off course.

I've lived in the Greater Milwaukee area all of my life. I know this town like the back of my hand. But get me out of town, and I can loose my way pretty quick. I'm also an optimist by nature, so I never say "I'm lost," I just got off track. I'm also a biker, riding my Harley is always about the journey, so everything becomes an adventure. The adventure can be dangerous when you don't rely on the Holy Spirit to help you be where you need to be in life.

I have a GPS that I call Lola. Lola is awesome. She tells me which way to turn, and how far I need to go, and will even tell me the approximate arrival time — IF I follow her directions. Sometimes she shows me off-roading, but she always knows where I am.

Lola will also recalculate over and over if I refuse to listen. You know how it is, sometimes we just know a short cut and bypass what Lola says. She doesn't get confused. She just recalculates. I love Lola. We work in tandem, me and Lola.

I don't want to sound disrespectful about the Holy Spirit. The Holy Spirit cannot even be compared to Lola. But how often do we treat the Holy Spirit like we do our GPS? If we get stuck, we really rely on its direction. Otherwise we just try to navigate ourselves. When we "off road", the Holy Spirit tries to tell us much like my Lola, "Re-calculating... make a u-turn at the next available opportunity...turn left at the corner and...Re-calculating." Yeah. It's like that with the Holy Spirit sometimes too.

The Spirit is IN us, that inner compass, or GPS. Sometimes we listen, sometimes we off-road, or go our own short cut. Those short cuts often turn out to be LONG cuts and we should have listened to the Spirit the first time around.

Our willingness to listen to the Spirit is directly connected to the depth of our relationship with God. Do I spend time with the one I love every day? Do I seek His instruction? Do I listen to His voice? Do I do what He tells me to do or try to short cut it?

A heart that desires to follow Him every day will pray for wisdom and direction knowing that in His Spirit is the path that leads to life. I will accomplish all that I need and receive the blessing and favor of God, if I listen to that inner voice of the Holy Spirit.

> **Our willingness to listen to the Spirit is directly connected to the depth of our relationship with God.**

Psalm 25:4-5 NIV "Show me your ways, O LORD, teach me your paths; guide me in your truth and teach me, for you are God my Savior, and my hope is in you all day long."

Sometimes, we can be such hard heads. He shows us, tells us and points us in the right direction. And we knowingly go the other way. God help us to put our hope in you "all day long." Help us to realize Your voice and direction, and follow You.

Proverbs 4:10-13 NIV "Listen, my son, accept what I say, and the years of your life will be many. I guide you in the way of wisdom and lead you along straight paths.

When you walk, your steps will not be hampered; when you run, you will not stumble. Hold on to instruction, do not let it go; guard it well, for it is your life."

Give me ears to hear. Jesus told us so many times, "let him that has ears to hear, hear." We've all got ears. Even if we are deaf, we have an inner compass and internal GPS in the Holy Spirit. Let us hear and do what He tells us. That dear ones, is where the blessing and favor of God lies. That is where our protection is, our safety, wisdom and instructions. Give us ears to hear.

So to go back to the original question: does God give His people an instinct? The answer is yes. The incredible Holy Spirit of God that lives IN us. Not only does He tell us the way, and help us to not stumble, but He gives us everything we need to live out every day as His Word tells us. I don't know about you, but that gives me a hope in a great future. The Holy Spirit, the "instinct", inner compass, GPS of the believer in **THIS PYRAMID**.

PRINCIPLE 3 - PURPOSE OF THE JOURNEY

The march that the penguins take annually is for one purpose: to produce offspring. They stay incredibly focused on the reason for the journey. Depending on the breed, some of them mate for life.

Another interesting parallel between the purpose of the penguin journey and that of the journey of the church is that both are for the purpose of producing offspring. Our main purpose in the Church is to take the good news to those who are lost, those with no relationship with the God that loves them and has a plan for their lives. God has prepared a way for us to show them the love of God, that they would see Him in us as His Holy Spirit shines through us. That our lives shine forth with the love and truth of our God. The scriptures tell us that it is the Spirit that draws them. All we need to do is be a light that can be seen and experienced. That they would accept Christ as their Lord and Savior, ask Him to forgive them and bring them into relationship with Him. And as they grow in Him, they too would produce offspring. **Time is short and eternity is long.** Are we accomplishing our purpose?

The early church understood this mission. There was no question that this was their purpose. We read accounts of the stand they took so others would find new life in Christ. Many laid down their very lives so that the lost would be saved. Today, there are many that are doing the same. The question I would pose here today is this: Do I have that same understanding of the purpose of the journey in Christ? Do I use every opportunity to reach the lost for Christ? Do I pray regularly for those that are lost without Christ? I would say that most of us get caught up in day-to-day life and we forget the reason for this journey.

There are many lost without Christ. The reason for this journey is to produce offspring. The penguins know their purpose. The challenge to us is this: Do we really get that? It's so easy to get caught up in the fact that God loves us (and He does), and we just revel in that and forget there is work to be done. It's just me and God - and we're good, so it's all good. No – there is work to be done. The reason the Spirit shines through every relationship is because there is work to be done. Our lives are to represent the fact that God loves people and will give us opportunity to reach them for Him.

There are other reasons that the church exists today: worship, prayer, relationship with God and others, service, study of the Word, and community involvement. But the main reason is not so that we can hunker in the bunker with those like us; being happy in the holy huddle. But rather the main purpose is that we produce offspring. Not offspring to be like us, but offspring to be like Jesus – Jesus followers. That is why it is critical that it is His light that shines through us. *1 Corinthians 11:1 NIV "Follow my example, as I follow the example of Christ." Do you and I live our lives like we really understand the purpose for the journey?*

Rick Richardson, in his great book on Evangelism, *Evangelism Outside the Box,* tells an incredible true story of the urgency of our day: the introduction sets the stage.

> *"When I was six years old, I got an unforgettable picture of God's heart. My dad was in the military, stationed in North Carolina. Across from our family's home lived a family also in the military. We had three boys. They had three girls. Each Friday in warm weather our moms drove the six kids an hour to the beach, where we spent the day building sand castles and wading in the waves. Then we would pile back into the big ugly green station wagon and return home.*
>
> *On one of our trips back home, with us in the middle of the fifteenth verse of the song about Noah's 'arky, arky', and the animals that came in by 'twosies, twosies', Allison, the youngest girl, asked where Chris was. Chris was my youngest brother, three years old. He was a trickster, so we thought he must be hiding somewhere in the car. We looked under the beach blankets. We looked in the tire well. We searched the back of the car. No Chris. He must still be at the beach.*

'Mom, Chris isn't here,' I reported.

'Wha-a-a-t?' My mother responded. At that moment I began the ride of my life! My mother hit the brake with magnum force. She spun that big ugly green station wagon in a 180-degree turn, tires screeching. Then she put the pedal to the metal. What had been a thirty-minute trip from the beach took us fifteen minutes going back. I think we hit a hundred miles per hour, and we only stayed that low because it was an old car and just couldn't go any faster.

At the beach we piled out and ran back through the archway and onto the sand. We ran from guard station to guard station. At the last one, my mother saw Chris and Chris saw my mother. They called out to each other. They ran toward each other. And then it was like a scene from a movie. My Mom caught Chris in her arms and twirled him, hugging him, laughing and crying all at the same time.

Chris was lost. My mother braved the curves of North Carolina roads and (it felt like) risked all our lives to find him. But that passionate mother-love for her lost child is only a glimmer of the passion that God has for those who are lost and don't know Jesus. He wants to turn the big, ugly green station wagon (maybe an appropriate analogy for our church or ministry) around and race to wherever those lost and hurting people can be found. But he's letting *us drive. We are at the steering wheel of the green station wagon. If we are happy with who is already in the car and who is not, we can continue on home singing our fun travel songs.*

God is looking for station wagon drivers who will collaborate with him to reach the lost and to fulfill the Great Commission."

Thanks Rick Richardson for such a great analogy. Again, a question for us: Do we sense with the same passion, the purpose for our journey – to reach the lost? Or to use penguin terms, produce offspring?

If we do, there is little to nothing that will stop us from reaching out to those that do not know Christ. We will be impassioned to do so. There is little to nothing that will stop the penguins from this march every year. Their instincts just take them to the breeding ground and the production of offspring. Do we have that same Holy Spirit passion to collaborate with God to fulfill the Great Commission, or the Purpose for the Journey?

As a good pastor friend of mine, Rev. Jerry Brooks says so often, and you've heard me quote him often: "Time is short and eternity is long." We must focus on the lost. We must pray for the lost and use every opportunity to share the good news that Jesus came to pay a price for their sin. That you and I would sense that same passion to reach them, to produce offspring, that the lost would be saved, and the Kingdom advanced.

That we would live our lives as **THIS PYRAMID** reflecting the Holy Spirit of the Living God to everyone in our sphere of influence. **That friends, is the purpose in the journey.**

PRINCIPLE 4 - PROTECTION OF THE OFFSPRING

Back to the penguins: Once the destination is reached and eggs produced, the males are dedicated to the care of the egg. He huddles that egg in a little pouch to protect it, right between his feet. He balances the egg to protect it from harsh weather and predators. If it slips away, he quickly recaptures it, to keep it warm. If he does not, the chick will freeze, or be stolen by a predator, and not survive.

The predators are lurking, looking for a loose egg to snatch up for a feast. The male works hard to protect that little chick.

While the dad is protecting the chick, the mom leaves to head back to the sea for food. She will travel for three months to reach the starting place. She's eager to get back into the water. As she searches for food, she is able to hold her breath for fifteen minutes and dive down one-thousand, five-hundred feet to find food. But there are also predators there. If a predator takes the life of the mom, it means the life of the child is also lost. She is the one to bring the food back for the chick.

The dads wait, keeping the chick safe and warm. They cling to life with their chicks under them, catching snowflakes to satisfy their thirst. The dads will go up to four months without food. They will maintain a small amount of milk in the pouch for the chick to feast on when the time is right. The dad will lose up to half of his own body weight during this time. Everything is reserved for the babe. Once the mom returns to feed the chick, then dad begins the seventy mile walk back for food. He is literally starving at this point, in dire need of nutrition. With the instinct that the penguins have, they know what to do. They understand that the chick will not survive without their great care and feeding and they will do whatever it takes for that to be so.

At that time, they are completely focused on caring for that chick, and little to nothing will dissuade them. The cost is too high if anything causes them to loose focus. If they fail, the chick dies. If they are not always on watch, they, and their chick, will be destroyed by predators. The responsibility is theirs and bailing out on their responsibility is simply never an option. They may die trying but never bale out.

Again, a question for us: Do we, the church, recognize the great responsibility that we have to train up the new believers in Christ? Years ago, there was an analogy about evangelism and discipleship that I never really liked very much. It was about catching and cleaning the fish. The saying was that first we catch them, and then we clean them. I didn't like it then, and I don't like it today. Why? I NEVER believed that Jesus taught us to clean the fish. Be an instrument that God uses to bring people to Him, but it's never our job to clean them. I don't have to clean up anyone, nor do you.

It is, however, our responsibility to take care, feed and nourish the new believers. To love them, protect them from predators, teach them about the great love of God and the incredible power of the Holy Spirit. They need to know that the Holy Spirit dwells in the life of every believer, including them, and gives them the power to walk in newness of life. And we do that until they are able to walk on their own, and enter into becoming producers of offspring themselves.

We can't miss this. The cost is too great for us to not grasp the seriousness of this principle. We have to UNDERSTAND the great responsibility to disciple new believers. If your life is a **THIS PYRAMID** life, this is in your DNA!

I remember when I was just twenty-two years old, I was surrounded by people that just loved me as a new believer. They invested in my life, and helped me to see my value to God and the Kingdom. I did some pretty bone headed things. I could have easily fallen back into my own sin and been a pretty hearty lunch for a predator. But they protected me. They taught me many scriptures, like:

John 10:10 NIV *"The thief comes only to steal and kill and destroy; I have come that they may have life, and have it to the full."*

They taught me to be aware that the predator was out there, the evil one, the devil who hates Christ followers, and to be on the lookout. They taught me how to put on my spiritual armor every day. They taught me how to communicate with my God first thing every morning. In today's culture, that whole "first thing every morning" thing is a very hard concept for people. Most often people get up, do their "first of the morning" routine and get started with their day. Or, many hit the snooze button on their alarms so many times that the only time they have is to brush their teeth, throw on their clothes, leaving just enough time to run out the door and in the car or at the bus stop to get to the job. Lord help them if there's a traffic jam somewhere, because they allowed no time for error.

I'm a morning person. I truly do enjoy my mornings, and do my best to make sure I have adequate time to do the things that I must before heading out the door. My morning routine is really quite simple. I do the normal things that everyone does in the morning. The kitchen is the next destination where I pull out the coffee beans, grind them, fill the pot with water, get it all set and turn on the coffee maker for that "heavenly beverage." Lord help the person that gets in the way of that routine.

There's probably someone thinking, "WHAT??? Wait. You mean you don't pick up the Word before you do anything????" I pick up the Word — I promise you I do. Though the predator tries to distract me from that too. After flipping the switch on my coffee maker, I head over to my "God spot." We have a huge over stuffed burgundy/purple sofa in our living room that is my God spot where He and I meet every morning for devotion time. Indeed my favorite place in my house. It's just for us, me and my God: my Savior, Redeemer and Friend.

You have to know this, cell phones and devotion times don't go well together, at least for me. If I pick up my cell phone BEFORE I have my devotions, it will not go well for me. The predators lurk in alerts. There will be all kinds of alerts going off: text alerts, Facebook alerts, email alerts, you name it. And I know myself well enough to know that once I allow that distraction, the day will go quite differently. So I have to discipline myself to leave the phone alone until I've had my devotion time with the Lord. Everything else can wait until I've had my time alone with my best friend.

There's nothing as awesome as my time on my big overstuffed couch with my God. I would say, there's nothing as good as Jesus and my cup of coffee in the morning. God loves our time together too. I know because He talks to me especially during those times.

> If I pick up my cell phone BEFORE I have my devotions, it will not go well for me. ***The predators lurk in alerts.***

Those dear sweet people that invested in me so many years ago also taught me to not give too much attention to that predator, the Devil. He is quite happy just to have me get my eyes off of Jesus long enough to put me in harms way, spiritually, physically, emotionally or whatever. Be aware of your predator, but don't invest all your time looking for him behind every door post. Stay focused on Jesus, the author and finisher of your faith.

Those Christians back then also provided for a safe environment for me and I always felt loved. They never judged or criticized me, or like some others would say "clean the fish". I'm so grateful that nobody ever thought they had to clean the mess in my life. Through their love and acceptance I was able to see the great love of God. I was able to see the great mercy and grace of God that didn't leave me feeling shamed, but rather I was able to face my own sin and allow Him to do a work that nobody but Him could do.

There is a big difference between feeling loved and feeling like someone's project. Nobody likes to feel like somebody's project. You can never measure up if you are someone's project. The penguin principle of **Protection and Growth of Offspring** never leaves an individual feeling like a project. But rather, knowing that God loves them, accepts them, and has a great plan for their lives. At the end of the day, you can always trust that His plans are to prosper you, to give you hope and a future.

Jeremiah 29:11-13 NIV "For I know the plans I have for you," declares the LORD, "plans to prosper you and not to harm you, plans to give you hope and a future. Then you will call upon me and come and pray to me, and I will listen to you. You will seek me and find me when you seek me with all your heart."

See, those that protect you and help you to grow, know that you need to learn to care for yourself. So they never let you get too attached to them, but always show you the way to Him. It's HIS plans that are great. It's Him that we seek. Not them.

One last thought on protection. The Christians in my life let the Holy Spirit do in me what only He can do. They didn't try to play His part. I remember well, one night, wandering off to someplace that I should not have gone. Some "old friends" invited my husband and I to go out for some drinking and drugging. "One last time," we said. "Surely God won't mind if we go out one last time." Didn't think twice about it — why? Because babes, penguin chicks or spiritual babes don't understand the danger involved. They just wander about. They're like two year old toddlers who get into trouble because they can't understand the dangers yet.

Thank God for His Holy Spirit. I remember vividly, just like it were yesterday. I was sitting at a high top table, beer in my hand, cigarette in the other, laughing it up with friends. My husband was outside smoking dope and drinking with friends. Seemingly out of nowhere, right in the middle of the band playing my favorite tune, I noticed the sign above the bar — "LUCIFERS", in blinking neon. The name of the bar had changed and we had no idea. Let me tell you. The Holy Spirit grabbed a hold of my heart and let me know that this was no longer my life. I squashed my cigarette, set down my beer and headed out the door, never to return. I saw Rick and said, "We gotta go. Like now!"

The believers in my life allowed God to do what only God could do. Just like those baby penguins, wandering away from safety, the protection of their father was right there to scoop them up from the predators that were stalking.

Loving, protecting and growing new believers in the faith is top priority; if we don't, they can be gobbled up by predators. The cost is too great. Their souls are at stake. Will you protect and grow those in your life?

PRINCIPLE 5 - WE'RE BLOOD

Major Crisis

Penguins endure horrible arctic winters. As they are waiting for the return of the females with food they huddle together to survive. Never do they try to do this alone. They realize they need each other if they are going to survive.

They form a big circle and every one of them finds a secure spot in that circle, fitting everyone in, so that no one is out there alone, freezing. You read earlier about how we did that in the ocean in Costa Rica, standing tightly together so we could stand the force of the waves together. Alone, we never would have survived it.

In a large circle of bodies, there are some on the inside of the huddle, the warmest place to be. There are also some on the outside of the huddle, the coldest place to be. They live every moment, shuffling, moving, slowly, rotating that circle in such a way that every one gets a chance to be in the middle where it's the warmest, and everyone gets to take their time in the cold, providing a barrier for the rest.

Working together, they all move slowly, in the same direction, everyone in survival mode, that none would be lost. If they don't, some would freeze to death and the loss of life is just unacceptable to the herd. So, together they survive the worst arctic weather.

As I watched that in the documentary, I couldn't help but wonder how we, God's people, the Body of Christ, respond to crisis? Do we pull together so that all survive? Do we argue about the best solutions to end the crisis? Do we push some away if they don't participate the way we think they should? Do we allow our circumstances to draw us together or do we use them to tear us apart?

We have been through some extremely difficult crisis in the church throughout the years. Some have drawn us together, and sadly, others have torn us apart. We pick sides like the world picks sides in an election or on a baseball or football team. We slam the other side; we trash talk like the world does when they disagree with a method or path.

I can tell you from experience, the times that brought incredible healing are the times that we drew together. When we chose to be tight, all for one and one for all, pulling together for the good of us all. That NOT ONE would be lost, hurt or pushed away. We were the body. Do I see you as more important than me? Or am I fighting for myself, and only thinking about MY good? To you, dear friend, are others a priority to you? Or are you focused on yourself? As family, we should be focused on us as whole, and not selfishly looking out for our own good.

In our family, we have used a well-known phrase when crisis hits: we're blood. We are family with common blood running through our veins. We also have the blood of Christ coursing through our veins, binding us tight as His Body. We are blood. Our focus should be on "us", and not selfishly focused on me as an individual. That's what "blood" does.

Will we, the Church, deal with crisis the same? The blessing and favor of God rests on us as a whole when we choose to live together in unity – we are blood. First and foremost, we are family. Blood is thicker than water. Or so we say.

The Worst Crisis

In the penguin world, the worst crisis of all is the loss of a chick. They try everything they know to revive a chick that might be struggling to survive the horrible arctic winter. When they are unsuccessful, the grief is horrible. The mother, in her incredible grief will do the unthinkable and try to steal a chick from one of the other mothers.

The group stands up and will not allow her to steal another's baby. They protect each other, including the mother and father with the great loss. They instinctively know that the parents have to work through their grief and give them the time they need to do that, without allowing them to cause unnecessary pain for another family.

Over the years, I have had the honor to be on several teams that follow up and disciple those new to the faith. Those that are "babes" in Christ, who need protection, leading, teaching, and direction in their new found faith. We do all we know to do. We feed them the Word, we pray for and with them, we love them, we invite them into fellowship with the family, and walk with them on the journey to experience new life in Christ. We help them learn to share their faith with others, as they follow Jesus' command to "make disciples."

Once in a while, we see one that chooses to walk away and go back to their old life. The things of the world, old habits or friends become more attractive than their new life in Christ. We see the enemy of our souls pulling them back, and the pain is great. We jump into gear, and pray for God's intervention, and we do everything we know. As with the penguins, the grief of one lost is awful. Many can't understand why the grief is so great. We understand that every moment counts. None of us is guaranteed tomorrow and the choices we make this side of heaven count for eternity. Every step toward Christ matters and every step backwards matters even more.

Remember the penguins? It is unthinkable that they might loose a young one. They will do everything they can for that babe. Do we? Will we? Or do we just let them go and fend for themselves? Sometimes I have this horrible feeling that we are sad, but just wave goodbye. And hope they come back some day.

If we do what Jesus would do, we would continue to love them. When an open door presents itself for us to have good conversation together, we share the truth of God's Word that He loves them and wants them back. He wants the relationship with them more than we do. I promise you that.

I've had so many family members come to me for prayer. I remind them often "God loves your loved one more than you. I promise He does." I think that nobody loves my kids or grandkids more than me, but truth be known, God does. That is why He gave His Son to pay the price for our sin — that we could have a relationship with them. Knowing and accepting that, I can trust them to His hands. That frees me to just love them. He knows what they need. He will give them what they need. His goodness will draw them back to Him. Crisis, should it come into their lives, will be used by God to reach them as well. God never wastes a hurt. Because His love is so great, He is forever calling them; forever orchestrating circumstances to draw them back into His loving care. Do what you know to do and trust Him with their souls.

We do our best to help them see His love, grace and mercy, and they are always able to see Him in us. That is exactly what the light of the Spirit shining in **THIS PYRAMID** is meant to do; that they would see Him.

The common phrase in parenting today is **Helicopter Parents**. Parents that fly in to take care of everything their children need, truly enabling them, showing them that they can survive in life without taking any responsibility for themselves. The parents continue to take the responsibility and the kids grow up thinking everyone owes them. They never learn to grow, only to be dependent on someone other than God.

As a **Christian Helicopter** pilot, we do pretty much the same. They never learn to seek God themselves or go to Him to find all they need. Instead, we fly our helicopters in and take care of everything for them. They end up seeking us and not God. We become responsible for their happiness, and they never really develop the relationship with God that He wants with them. We continue to feel drained, and they have a false sense of fulfillment, only it's in YOU and not God. When they have to stand alone, they will die empty and dry, because they have never learned to go to the source of the Living Water to be filled. We must raise them to live independent of us.

Independent and striving to be all they are meant to be, yet dependent on the Body, because together, we are better.

Yes, we are "blood." The blood of Christ coursing through our veins, a visual to those in our sphere of influence that He is alive. He is our source. He is our life. Together, we stand strong. Together, the world sees Him in us. Together, tight as the penguins in the circle, to keep each other warm and healthy we stand. With all our warts and pimples, different as night and day, one race, the human race, with every nationality, tribe, tongue and color of skin and hair. We are the body of Christ, imperfect people, but our righteousness is found in Christ.

In **THIS PYRAMID**, the shining, radiant, shimmering light of the Holy Spirit shines in and through every relationship in our lives.

"If you are filled with light, with no dark corners, then your whole life will be radiant, as though a floodlight were filling you with light." Luke 11:36 MSG

What a picture: "as though a floodlight were filling you with light." Solid on the foundation of the Father, Son and Holy Spirit, that Spirit shining up through every relationship: marriage, family, friends, neighbors, co-workers, hobby partners, Church friends and everything I may have missed. The Holy Spirit's floodlight seeping through every layer of relationship – with a power beam coming out through each, for all the world to see. A picture of a Christian life: founded in Him, reflecting His image in every layer of relationship in your life.

It doesn't get any better. Is that light shining in every relationship in your life? Or do you need help in one layer or another? Whether it's marriage, family, or church family, the answer to any dull or missing light is found in the foundation. Go back. Go back to the foundation chapter in Part One. When the foundation is right, every other area becomes a reflection of our relationship with Him.

As life happens, we struggle. We go back to what we know. We go back to the Word, to the foundation that is secure. That light that comes from Him, illuminates in our heart once again to reveal truth. So daily we seek Him. Daily we find Him. Daily we reflect His image to the world.

"Seek the Lord while you can find him. Call on him now while he is near." Isaiah 55:6 NIV

"...let your light shine before others, that they may see your good deeds and glorify your Father in heaven." Matthew 5:16 NIV

"You will seek me and find me when you seek me with all your heart." Jeremiah 29:13 NIV

"Blessed are those who keep his statutes and seek him with all their heart" Psalm 119:2 NIV

"But if we walk in the light, as he is in the light, we have fellowship with one another, and the blood of Jesus, his Son, purifies us from all sin."
I John 1:7 NIV

LAURIE GANIERE

PART FOUR
Especially Difficult People

LAURIE GANIERE

PEOPLE ARE THE WAY THEY ARE FOR A REASON

In this last part of **THIS PYRAMID**, I want to take a few pages and talk about the light of the Holy Spirit and what happens in difficult or fractured relationships. Can the light of the Holy Spirit continue to shine? If so, how? If not, can we accept the fact that it is us that squelches the Spirit in those relationships? How do we reconcile that thought with a God that loves all people and asks us to do the same?

I talked earlier about abuse, and the necessity to put distance between the abuser and the victim. In many abusive relationships, it's simply not safe to continue to put ourselves in the path of dangerous behavior. Only God can heal the abuser, so we walk in forgiveness and move on. That's not unforgiveness, that's healthy boundaries.

Most relationship problems, though, are not abusive. Most friendship breakups or family fractures involve expectations that we have of others. When they don't meet our expectations, we shut them down, say bad things to them, and even encourage others to do the same. Or we huddle in our own protective world and shut them out. We can even get down right self-righteous about it, and claim that God told us to shut down the relationship. That's a bit contradictory to the Word of God which tells us to live at peace with all men, and that we are the light of the Word to reflect the glory of God.

Many of the ancient pyramids were designed to use the most precious materials at the top for all to see. As the sun shone on those precious materials, they were brilliant and beautiful. I would suggest that maybe, just maybe, difficult relationships might be the best opportunity for the Holy Spirit to shine the brightest at the top of **THIS PYRAMID** as well. I would also suggest this: People are the way they are for a reason.

When people treat us poorly, or we're ticked at how they act, sometimes we need to stop and consider that people are the way they are for a reason. I'm not saying that to make excuses for bad behavior, but sometimes, we have to understand the simple principle that people are the way they are for a reason and give them grace when they deserve a high five to the forehead. That's what Jesus does for us, doesn't He?

I heard an athlete say recently that people see him today and applaud what he does. They don't have any idea where he has come from. They have no idea of the struggles he had to overcome. I thought about that relative to so many others that we might be impatient with, or those that we think should "know better." We see what we see and what's on the surface, but don't see where they've come from. People are the way they are for a reason. We don't know what's going on in someone's life. We really don't know their struggles, yet we expect them to act according to expectations we have for them, according to what we feel they should be. When those expectations are not met, when they don't respond to us in a way we think they should, we shut them out, or shut them down, or self-righteously, Pharisee like, turn our backs on them.

Jesus loved me enough to not do that with me. He continually pulled me close so that I began to trust Him to do what only He could do. Thankfully, I had some people in my life that did the same. They were truly Jesus with skin to me. But, then there were others who were quick to judge my actions or words, and embarrass me in front of others. All because I didn't live up to their expectations of what my Christian walk should look like. They had no idea what I was going through or had gone through. The question I have asked for years is, "Who are we to judge?" Seems we're told that in the Word too. Judge not or we will be judged. We are told to be patient with others, to love them and show grace, mercy, and extend the love of Christ to them always. Always!

I said all that to say this: sadly, we have expectations of people that are not ours to have. People are the way they are for a reason. God takes us all from where we are to the next place. Shouldn't we give people the same grace?

My dad left this earth over twenty years ago. To say he was sometimes a difficult man would be an understatement. I always knew my dad loved me, my brother Ron, and my mother. I always knew he loved his grandkids and daughter-in-law and son-in-law. But he had little grace for others and at times, he had little grace for us either.

For so many years, he pushed people out of his life; always found things wrong with them and severed those relationships. That left him and my mother isolated up in the north woods of Minnesota. My mom still worked, so she had some interaction with people. That, along with her faith in Christ, was her lifeline. Even when I saw him verbally slam so many good people I was sure that he would never do the same to me. I was wrong, the time came that he did.

My family and I were visiting my parents home, as we did several times a year. We had been there for almost a week. I was VERY pregnant with our fourth child. My dad's paranoia was in full swing. He was sure everyone was trying to destroy something of his. He had been angry most of the day and it came into full blows during dinner. He said some horrible things to my kids who were way too young to know what was going on. One was nine, another seven, and the youngest was just four. I flew into protection mode. I knew I had to protect my family from his rage. He never had physical rage, but verbal was another thing. We made plans to leave that night.

I left dinner and drove to the nearest resort to make a call to my cousin Don who lived a few hours away in northwestern Wisconsin. He invited us to come and spend the evening with them. I went back to my folks house where Rick had already had the kids packing up to leave.

After I had the kids settled down in the car, I made up some dumb story about why we had to leave so quickly. We drove to my cousin Don's home. He and his wife and family were pastoring in a small town just across the river from Minnesota in Wisconsin. I'll tell you, their home was a refuge. They helped us get our emotional bearings back so we could continue travel the next day. I was so very grateful for the love they showed us. They even took us to do something fun the next day to get our minds off of the crisis in the family. It was such a gracious gift toward us from them.

Eventually our relationship was restored with my dad, years later. When he invited us back there, I went alone. I did not want to subject my family to another visit until I knew it was safe. I'll get to the results of that trip later in this story.

There were many wonderful memories with my mom and dad, but there were so many hard ones as well. I had no idea why he was the way he was. Because he pushed so many people out of his life, he wasn't close to many people, including his seven brothers. I could never understand why. Even when three of them died, he felt no need to go to their funerals saying, "I was never close to those people." I was somewhat incensed. "Those people?

They are your brothers." You see, growing up, they never had the opportunity to develop relationships as siblings should.

THE OSELAND YEARS

Dad grew up during very hard times in the early 1900's. His parents were both immigrants from Norway. They came here with dreams of making a good life. They married when they landed here in the US. His parents began having children shortly after they were married, and ended up with eight sons, and a continual struggle to provide. Life was very hard. My grandfather, who I never knew, worked the railroads when my dad was very young. Dad told me he had memories of meeting his dad after work at the railroad, to carry his lunch pail home. One of the few good memories he had.

When my grandparents, Abraham and Hannah, were able, they bought a farm, as farming was something they knew would help them provide for their family. My grandfather came from a very large family farm in Norway, which still stands today. My grandparents suffered a horrible catastrophe when they lost their farm. First they lost their cattle through a wasting disease of some sort, followed by a fire that took everything they had. It was almost more than either one of them could take. My grandfather began suffering from depression and became extremely paranoid. At some point, his paranoia pushed my grandma over the edge and she too had a nervous breakdown.

Abraham ended up in a hospital and died while there. My dad was just a young tike. As an adult, he was always so protective of the story of his dad's death. If anyone would bring it up he would get angry and almost belligerent if it was suggested that his dad had been in a mental institution. He said they were wrong and they didn't know what they were talking about. I never understood why he got so angry. There was never any information that we were privy to and dad wasn't giving any details.

I always knew my grandmother, Hannah, to be a beautiful Norwegian woman filled with humility and grace. I also knew she was left to raise eight sons alone. Not knowing the whole story, I was led to believe that the pressures and stresses of her life, with little money and a big family left her devastated. She battled with thoughts that she didn't have what it took to raise these sons alone. She was in a new country, away from her family support, without her husband and she then had a nervous breakdown.

As an adult, my dad was so very protective of his mother. Though she didn't live with us, dad had always planned to build her a house on a tree-lined lot. I

147

remember as a child, out on a Sunday drive, dad showing me the kind of lot he would love to buy to build a house for his mother. He was never able to build her that house, but he gave her what was in his power to give: the dignity, respect and grace that she deserved. He also helped with her physical needs where he could.

Another thing that angered dad was stories of how my Grandma Hannah lived during the time of their family separation. You see, all the boys, except one, were all taken from her. Two of them went into a Christian orphanage in Chicago, the rest were taken in by farmers to work their farms and stay with their families. The family was broken up. Dad would get so angry and say people had big mouths about things they knew nothing about. Because there was so much we didn't know, we would just be quiet and let him vent. Never asking any questions because that just made him more angry. Later, we learned that his mother lived much like a pauper for many years, never feeling that she deserved anything good. I remember her scrubbing floors just to put food on her table and living in rooming houses, away from her family. Enjoying what little time she did get with them. As she grew older, we did have her in our home for a while.

For so many years I cherished a picture of my grandma Hannah and all eight of her sons. My dad was about eleven or twelve in that picture. I was delighted to one day have it restored and make copies for my brother and I, and especially my dad. With great pride I presented him with the picture. I was shocked when dad was not happy to see that picture. He put it down, upside down and said he didn't want to see that picture. I was devastated. This was our history! This was part of the story of our family! It was a great treasure to me, one of the only pictures of dad, his brothers and mother.

To my dad, it meant something altogether different. What I didn't know was that it reminded him of a painful family history most of which he had never shared with anyone. At the time, I was crushed at the thought that he really didn't want anything to do with the picture. Once again, sounding like a broken record, people are the way they are for a reason. I didn't know the reasons.

With a wee bit of fear and trembling, I asked dad why he didn't like that picture. He said, "It brings back nothing but bad memories." I asked him, "What bad memories? To me it looks like such a great family photo." He went on to tell me that all the boys and grandma were brought to the "cities" (Minneapolis/St. Paul), and had to all get dressed up for the picture. I wish you could have seen the hurt and anger in his face telling me this. It is emblazoned in my mind to this day.

Dad went on to say that after the pictures were finished, all of the boys were yanked back away from each other, and sent back to the work farms, away from their brothers and mother. They could not spend any time together. His little heart was broken. He told of how sad it was standing at that train station, knowing he may never see any of them again. Did I tell you that he was just a kid? He was just a kid! I began to understand. I wipe away tears today just thinking about it. People are the way they are for a reason.

Some time later, I asked dad to tell me some stories from him growing up. I told him that it was our family history, and I wanted to know how all the dots connected. I didn't realize what I was asking. His response to me was, "just the good stuff, Lor. That's what I'll tell you. Just the good stuff." I was quick to say, "No dad, not just the good stuff. Everything. Those things made you the man you are today. I want to know the good, the bad and the ugly! That's what makes us who we are." He sat silent. He gave me no response. Stared into space like he often did when I asked questions like that.

Please know that there were some stories that we all heard throughout the years. The funny stories were the ones about the Oseland boys and all the trouble they got into. Stories of life on the farms of the families they worked for. Remember, they were just kids. One such story was about how the farmer's wife had all of her lady friends over for an afternoon card party. Dad said the ladies were all dressed up sitting in the "parlor," playing cards. My dad and his brother, Art, took a bull out of the barn and managed to get him up on the porch. Don't ask me how they got it up there without anyone hearing, but they did. Then they opened the door and twisted that bull's tail so that he ran right in to the middle of that ladies card party. Dad would laugh himself silly reliving it every time he re-told it. I'm sure there was hell to pay, but it sounded like life wasn't all that good, so the hell to pay for the bull was probably worth the entertainment.

Other than a few stories like that, we didn't know much. There was one story though that dad told me time after time after time after time. I used to wonder what it was about that story that he felt he had to keep repeating it. It was about how he was just eight years old, after his dad had died, but before the family was broken up. One day, he was out in a field, with rocks all around. There was a bird stuck in a rock and he was working hard to get the bird loose. His brother came to get him, to tell him that mom wanted him home. He shooed his brother away, telling him that he had something important to take care of. Because my dad loved wild life, I thought the story was about the bird that was stuck, and he worked feverishly to get it loose. But there was much more to the story.

A short time later, another brother came. "Harry, mom wants you home NOW." Again, my dad got angry with him and shooed him away. He had something more important to deal with. Soon, the brothers stopped coming and he was left to deal with the bird. He stayed there until he got the rock lifted enough to release that little bird. That's it.

That's the story. Over and over and over again, for years, I heard this same story.

As I said, I believe people are the way they are for a reason. I just had not discovered quite why my dad was the man he was because I hadn't heard the whole story.

Remember I said I took a trip up there alone, after dad invited us up? Well, during that time up there, dad and I went for a drive in my mom's Bronco II. We left with dad driving, and after we were out on the road, dad smiled and told me to slide over and drive. It was mom's truck and she let NO ONE drive it, not even me. During that drive, dad started to tell me that story again. Inside I was ready to check out. I'd heard the same story so often I could tell it by myself. But then something happened. Dad continued talking about what happened after he released that bird. My ears perked and what I heard next made a lot of things start to make sense. It was horribly sad, but now so many things made sense. Why the picture was so painful, why he didn't want to talk about family history, why he was the man he was. It was about to get real folks.

Dad said when he was done with the bird, he went home, walked in the door and the scene he found was unbelievable, like a nightmare. Grandma Hannah had a nervous breakdown and caused harm to herself and the other children. Dad saw the horrifying scene and ran with all his might, as fast as his little eight year old legs could carry him to the farm way down the road to get help.

A lot began to make sense after that. Why Dad was so protective of grandma. Why dad got so angry when people told the story. None of those people were there. They knew nothing. Why dad was so protective of his own family, mom and us kids. A lot made sense. My heart breaks at the thought of the weight of what that eight year-old saw, and carried all of his life. Had he come home when he was summoned that day, they all would have very well been dead. My dad, through the grace of God, saved his family that day. But nobody knew that; nobody, but him, the people that came to help, and God. My heart broke at the incredible weight that he carried for all those years. It was partially responsible for making him the man he was.

One of the things my dad also had little grace for was church folks. After the boys were removed out of my grandmother's care, as I said, they were put on the work farms of other families; many who claimed to be Christians. They were treated so badly that dad decided early in life that being a Christian meant being like those church people and he wanted nothing to do with being like that. It took him until years later before he came to faith in Christ. It wasn't until a few years before his death that he called to tell me "Lor, I made peace with my maker. Your ma told me you'd want to know." I can tell you where I was standing when I got that phone call. God be praised. I prayed for my dad for years and years, believing that God would get a hold of his heart. And that He did.

I tell you all of this to say, **people are the way they are for a reason**. God knows them. God knows their story. God knows when they will hear His voice and respond to Him.

What is in someone's past has everything to do with how they are today. Because we don't know what's in their hearts, our job is to patiently, love them as Christ loved us. When he finally told me some of the pain he held in for so many years, I, for the first time in my life, began to understand and love my dad deeper than I had ever before.

I've had so many people in my office or across a table with coffee in hand tell me of their struggles with difficult relationships. Please know that people are the way they are for a reason. My heart breaks for people when they work so hard to change those people in their lives they think are broken. I am saddened that so many cut off family members just because in their estimation they "don't act right." We have troubled relationships and demand that people fix what we see as broken before we will have anything to do with them. How dare we? That is not how God treats us.

God gives us what we need, not what we deserve. He always gives us grace and mercy. How is it we don't extend that same grace and mercy to others? The closer relationally people are to us the harder we are on them.

We have expectations that are not ours to have. If they are family, we often are even harder on them.

So what should we do? Sow mercy into every relationship in our life. We don't know why people are the way they are, and we can't possibly know what they need. Because of that, our job is to sow seeds of mercy and grace.

Micah 6:8 "He has shown you, O mortal, what is good. And what does the Lord require of you? To act justly and to love mercy and to walk humbly with your God."

In being willing to show grace and mercy, we have to understand and accept that people are the way they are for a reason. You and I have no right to judge the reason. Some people come through extremely difficult things in their lives that have made them into the people they are. We have no right to judge and demand that they fix what is broken. That's God's job and I'm not God, nor are you.

A very difficult thing for a pastor is to give someone Godly counsel and have someone walk out of their office and walk back into the same mess they are working to get out of. Why? Not because they aren't listening to us. But rather, because we know the pain and agony they will continue to go through on their journey in life. We know the cycle will continue until they make some tough decisions. Until the pain they are living in becomes greater than their fear of change, they will never make those tough decisions. So what do we do in the mean time?

Prayerfully we do what Jesus would do. We love them anyway, and pick them up when they fall. We brush them off, pull them close, give them Godly counsel again, and just try to be Jesus with skin.

It's no different for any of us. We must do the same. We must not lose patience with them. Rather, just continue to show grace, love and mercy. As much as it depends on me, I must live at peace with them. Remember I said earlier that I would never give anyone a chance to say I dumped on them. I must never give them reason. Because Jesus will never, I must never. So I run to Him to give me the continual flow of love, grace and mercy for them. Then and only then will I have the ability to live at peace with all of them! No longer trying to fix them, giving them to God, and continuing to show love, grace and mercy.

> *If you judge people, you have no time to love them.*
>
> *People are unreasonable, illogical, and self-centered. Love them anyway.*
>
> **Mother Theresa**

Romans 12:18 NIV "If it is possible, as far as it depends on you, live at peace with everyone."

Philippians 4:13 NIV "I can do all this through him who gives me strength."

2 Corinthians 3:11 NIV "Strive for full restoration, encourage one another, be of one mind, live in peace. And the God of love and peace will be with you."

I do believe that the light of the Holy Spirit in *THIS PYRAMID* shines brightest in these most difficult relationships. Give them grace. Strive to live in peace. You be the one to show grace and mercy. Extend the olive branch. The blessing and favor of God is on us when we do. God be with you friends. Be a blessing to everyone in your sphere of influence.

Make sure your foundation is firmly in Christ, and let that light of His Spirit shine in every relationship in your life.

Matthew 5:16 NIV "In the same way, let your light shine before others, that they may see your good deeds and glorify your Father in heaven."

CLOSING THOUGHTS

It's so hard to close this book. For me at least!
I've spent a fair amount of time praying that you will
understand the need for your relationship with God to be
sure. That in Him you would find everything you need.
That you would see that His Spirit will shine through
you in every relationship in your life: **THIS PYRAMID** -
your marriage, your family, church family, co-workers,
neighbors, and anyone else in your sphere of influence.
God is willing. He's calling us to give every relationship
to Him. That you and I would step back, and allow that
precious Holy Spirit to do what only He can do IN us and
THROUGH us.

MY PRAYER FOR YOU:

Father God, I pray for my friends. I ask first of all that
they realize fully that their relationship with You is founded
on Your one and only Son, sent to this world to save us
from our sin. That in their relationship with You, Your Holy
Spirit would shine through them into everyone in their
lives. God give them a hunger and thirst for Your Word
and a fresh drink from Your well every day, that they would
seek You before anything or any one else. That nothing
would come between You and them. Let Your forgiveness

continue to shine that it washes away any hint of shame that would keep them from You. Bless them I pray, and that they find satisfaction in that blessing that it drives them to walk in obedience to You in all things.

In their marriages: that they would begin to see their spouse as Your gift to them. Give them all they need to show Your grace, mercy and love, even in the most difficult times. Remind them to be the first to say, "I'm sorry, please forgive me." Help them to see that Your Spirit shines brightest during those times of struggle. Help them to sow seeds of mercy and have the patience to wait for those seeds to grow and produce a harvest. Help them to see that they have a choice every day to sow seeds of grace and mercy. Remind them that the choice is theirs. Allow them just enough trials that they keep their eyes on You. Let them experience Your strength, support and victory as they walk together in the plans You have for them.

In their families: Father, give my friends the heart after Yours that they will set down their own pride and work with You to mend family relationships. Help my friends to let past hurts go. Give them the strength to not try to untangle things in the past, but to just let them go unto You. That they would walk in forgiveness and do all they know to show love, grace and mercy, by the power of Your

Spirit coming through them like a conduit. Help them be the first to say, "I'm sorry. Can we just start over?" Give them Your peace and Your love to shine through this layer of **THIS PYRAMID** to their families. That healing would begin in their hearts first, and radiate out to the others. For those that have good family relationships, help them to always speak in the love of Christ and always be an example of Your grace and mercy. Help them to always prefer others over themselves.

In their Church families: God I pray for peace in Your Church. This is Your body. We are but one part of that body. Help my friends to see the beauty of the body of Christ and fall in love with the differences between us. Help them to prefer each other and let the light of Your Holy Spirit to shine through them. God, I know You have told us so much in Your Word about the church. We have a tendency to expect more out of each other than we have a right to. Consequently, we judge when it's not our right to judge. Forgive us for standing in judgment of our brothers and sisters. Help us to always show grace and mercy, no matter our differences. Help us to rally together and be the example to the world that You intended. Your Word tells us that they would know us by our love. Help us to love and support each other in a way that brings You honor. Help us to protect each other from the evil one, that would rob, kill and destroy. Help us to see that we are Your family and Your blood runs through our veins; the blood of Jesus. Help us God to love each other the same way that You love us.

The light of the Spirit shines brightest at the top:
God for those that have struggled so, I ask for an extra measure of Your mercy. God help them to see that others are they way they are, mostly for reasons that they have no understanding. That it is You that will give them what they need, and the time frame necessary to accomplish Your will in those lives. Help them to always walk in mercy. That when it gets especially hard, that they keep their eyes on You, the author and finisher of their faith. Let Your love pour out on my friends, that love that is so deep, so wide, completely immeasurable, flooding their souls. God You have a plan to use them. You never waste a hurt. Help them to trust You, even with the most difficult.

It's Your light, Your Holy Spirit, residing in us, for all to see. Father, that we would always be found faithful. We give You praise. We give You honor. We give You glory.

In Jesus name.

Amen!

LAURIE GANIERE

NOTES AND REFERENCES

Introduction
- Luke 11:36 MSG

Part One – Foundation
- 1 Corinthians 3:16 NIV; Luke 11:36 MSG

Relationship with God
- Ephesians 2:8-9 NIV; Romans 3:23 NIV; Romans 6:23 NIV; John 3:16-17 NIV

My Story
- Jeremiah 29:11-13 NIV
- Michael Jr. Father's Day Video – "Open Your Eyes"

Foundation in Every Day Life
- Luke 6:47-49 NLT

God Given Needs
- Romans 8:38 NLT; Jeremiah 1:5 NLT; Hebrews 11:1-2 NLT

Faithsquasher No. 1 - Fear
- 2 Timothy 1:7 NKJV

Faithsquasher No. 2 - Comparison
- Robert Madu – "Comparison will consistently cloud the clarity of God's call on your life."
- 2 Corinthians 10:12 NIV
- Craig Groeschel's book: *#struggles*
- James 3:14-16 NLT

Faithsquasher No. 3 – Unforgiveness
- Matthew 6:14-15 NLT; Matthew 18
- Jeanne Mayo – "Unforgiveness is allowing a person to live in your head rent free."
- Laurie Ganiere-ism: "Unforgiveness corrodes the container that carries it."
- Drs. Henry Cloud and John Townsend's book: *Boundaries*
- RT Kendall's books: *Total Forgiveness* and *How to Totally Forgive Yourself*

Faithsquasher No. 4 – Looking for Love in all the Wrong Places
- "Open your eyes. I love you. Let me be the firm foundation in your life. I promise you - you and I will walk this road together. You will shine brightly with my strength, wisdom and power. You will affect everyone and everything in your sphere of influence. Why? Because your life will reflect Me. I love you. Open your eyes."

Part Two – Marriage and Family

Marriage Matters
- Ecclesiastes 1:9 NIV; Ecclesiastes 5:5 NIV; Romans 8:28 NIV; Proverbs 5:22 NIV; Proverbs 11:14 NIV

The Beginning
- Matthew 15:18 NIV; Proverbs 17:27 NIV; Proverbs 16:24 NIV; Ephesians 4:29 NIV

The Words Filter
- 2 Corinthians 10:5

So What's all This Talk About Submission
- Ephesians 5:21 NIV; Ecclesiastes 4:12 NIV

Cohabitation Before Marriage
- *Fireproof Your Marriage* – article by Mike and Harriet McManus, authors of *Living Together: Myths, Risks, and Answers*.

Unbelieving Spouse
- 2 Corinthians 7:14 NIV

Fight for Your Family
- Nicky Cruz's book *One Holy Fire,* chapter entitled: *Battle for the Family*
- Rev. Tony Whitley - Revival message, summer of 2016: "Taking Back the Streets"
- Mother Theresa – "If you want to change he world, go home and love your family."

Men and Respect
- Dr. Emerson Eggerich's book: *Love and Respect*

Abuse
- Rev. Gwen Tackett: Curriculum *Vessels of Honor*

Divorce
- www.divorcecare.org

Death
- www.griefshare.org

Part Three – The Penguin Principles
- *March of the Penguins*, released January 2005, Directed by Luc Jacquet

Principle 1   Church Family and other Close Relationships
- They need each other, depend on each other, fight for each other, go without so that their kids can survive, band together during storms, and work together

Principle 2 - Instinct
- Luke 12:12 NIV; John 16:13 NIV; 1 Samuel 15:22 NLT; 2 Corinthians 10:12 NIV; Psalm 25:4-5 NIV; Proverbs 4:10-13 NIV
- Our willingness to listen to the Spirit is directly connected to the depth of our relationships with God. Laurie Ganiere

Principle 3 – Purpose of the Journey
- "Time is short and eternity is long." Rev. Jerry Brooks
- 1 Corinthians 11:1 NIV
- Rick Richardson's book: *Evangelism Outside the Box*

Principle 4 – Protection of the Offspring
- John 10:10 NIV
- Jeremiah 29:11-13 NIV

Principle 5 – We're Blood
- Luke 11:36 MSG; Isaiah 55:6 NIV; Matthew 5:16 NIV; Jeremiah 29:13 NIV; Psalm 119:2 NIV; 1 John 1:7 NIV

Part Four _ Especially Difficult People
- Mother Theresa – "If you judge people, you have no time to love them. People are unreasonable, illogical, and self-centered. Love them anyway."
- Micah 6:8; Romans 12:18 NIV; Philippians 4:13 NIV; 2 Corinthians 3:11 NIV; Matthew 5:16 NIV

Made in the USA
Middletown, DE
25 January 2017